The Invasion of the
COMPUTER CULTURE

What You Need to Know
about the New World We Live In

**Allen Emerson
Cheryl Forbes**

INTERVARSITY PRESS
DOWNERS GROVE, ILLINOIS 60515

InterVarsity Press is the book-publishing division of InterVarsity Christian Fellowship, a student movement active on campus at hundreds of universities, colleges and schools of nursing. For information about local and regional activities, write Public Relations Dept., InterVarsity Christian Fellowship, 6400 Schroeder Rd., P.O. Box 7895, Madison, WI 53707-7895.

Distributed in Canada through InterVarsity Press, 860 Denison St., Unit 3, Markham, Ontario L3R 4H1, Canada.

All Scripture quotations, unless otherwise indicated, are from the Holy Bible, New International Version. Copyright © 1973, 1978, International Bible Society. Used by permission of Zondervan Bible Publishers.

Cover illustration: Robert Roper

ISBN 0-87784-515-8

Printed in the United States of America ∞

Library of Congress Cataloging-in-Publication Data

Emerson, Allen, 1937-
    The invasion of the computer culture: what you need to know about
the new world we live in/Allen Emerson, Cheryl Forbes.
      p.   cm.
    ISBN 0-87784-515-8
    1. Computers—United States.   2. Computers and civilization.
3. Artificial intelligence.   4. Neural circuitry.   I. Forbes,
Cheryl.   II. Title.
QA76.5.E558   1989
303.48'34—dc20
                                    89-31812
                                    CIP

16	15	14	13	12	11	10	9	8	7	6	5	4	3	2	1
99	98	97	96	95	94	93	92	91	90	89					

To the memory of
William John Emerson,
a craftsman
who knew how things worked,
and to
Nancy Elizabeth Emerson,
an artist
who sees why.

1
DISCOVERING
THE COMPUTER
MENTALITY

What is human? What is mind? These are weighty, age-old questions, once the stomping ground of philosophers, theologians and artists. No longer. The professionals of today who think about these questions are computer scientists—and cognitive psychologists who use the computer as a model of the mind. These people are revolutionizing society, not just in how we do science and commerce but even in how we think. And these are the people giving credence to a new way of thinking about the world we live in—the computer mentality.

What is the computer mentality? It is a world view inspired by computers and artificial intelligence. It sees intelligence and mind as dynamic streams of data, which it seeks to create or simulate. It assumes that humanity is the director of its own destiny and potentially the designer of minds more powerful than our own. The computer mentality, as we use the term, ignores or denigrates the belief that humanity is made in the image of God and insists that program is the measure of all things.

However, we didn't meet the computer mentality in such abstract, philosophical terms; we met it as parents concerned about the amount of time our children were spending with video games. Although we knew little about these games, we noticed that after playing them the children's personalities seemed changed. They became short-tempered, impatient and withdrawn. They were restless, too, as if the real world were no match for the exciting world of video games.

We thought about these games and talked about them over meals and long evenings. The more we talked and thought, the more concerned we became. What were they teaching our children about memory, thinking, success, power, human nature? Fortunately, our children have passed the video-game phase, and the video-game craze itself seems to have waned. Yet the questions we asked about video games also apply to their grown-up counterparts: computers.

Toys Meet Technology

At times we wondered if we were overreacting to a clever toy. But as any child psychologist will explain, toys are the work of children. Toys influence a child's behavior and personality. Give children the wrong toys and suffer the consequences, we're warned.

Indeed, computer programmers and toymakers have teamed to bring us sophisticated creatures; what was only a dream three years ago is now commerce. A report filed by Associated Press about the International Toy Fair explains:

> Parents may soon be hearing strange voices coming from their children's room at night.
>
> There's no cause for alarm, [sic] it's just dolls chatting. . . . [They] not only talk, they answer intelligently and carry on entire conversations among themselves.
>
> "We see the area of growth in true interactive toys," says Rick Anguilla, editor of the trade publication *Toy and Hobby World.* "Not just toys that have something to say and randomly say it, but those that almost seem to think and can have real conversations."[1]

The news release goes on to say that we can put two of these $100 dolls in a room, push their buttons, and they will sense each other's presence and begin talking—about ice cream, for example (they have preferences). Children can enter into the conversation at any time. Moreover, "These new dolls know what's going on all around them. Take them for a bumpy car ride and the doll might say, 'OK, that's enough. All this bouncing up and down makes me dizzy.' Kiss the doll's cheek, and it will say, 'Thank you for the kiss. May I have another one, please?' "

These dolls can sing together or tell a story as a team. One doll is capable of maturing "verbally and aesthetically from a 6-month-old to a 2-year-old, responding in turn to a child's voice and touch." These toys will have a much greater hold on children than video games had on our sons, because the dolls will seem so like humans.

Toys and games are only a small, albeit lucrative, part of the larger field of computers. We wondered if computers hinder imaginative thinking, making it difficult for children to understand or be affected by metaphorical language or parables and paradoxes or ideas that cannot be reduced to patterns of yes/no, right/wrong or off/on.

Of course, not everyone involved in computers or computer research has such a linear approach to thinking. In fact, some educators believe that computers teach children flexibility. Seymour Papert, the inventor of LOGO, the standard computer language for most elementary classrooms, wants computers to teach children abstractions, complexities and the concept of "there's more than one right answer." The result will be the development of problem-solvers—kids who can find things that go wrong. But again the emphasis here is on solutions and well-defined contexts in which solutions are possible.

The Big Picture

If this is what children come to understand about life—that there is always a solution to any problem, which can be reduced to either/or—how will they deal with the vagaries of being human? How will they understand the Bible, which is a book rich with metaphors, parables and paradoxes? How will they deal with Jesus—with the Incarnation, miracles, the Resurrection, none of which can be reduced to computer code? How will a computer handle such a theological concept as "This also is Thou; neither is this Thou." What about the children who are raised on—or by—computers?

Success can come easily, as can power. Children can control a game or program, whereas they cannot control their parents, siblings, friends or surroundings. A conquered computer program is a world that belongs solely to the conqueror. If a person just knows the right steps, he or she can succeed and needs no one else to help. Where, we wondered, do such important biblical concepts as community fit in?

So our thinking went. It had become apparent to us that the issues are far broader than our children's passing fancy with video games. As we read, we discovered that others had made the connection between video games and computers and had also realized that video games were just the tip of the computer iceberg. They were likewise concerned with the psychological and philosophical effects these machines have, not only on children, but on adults as well.

As we moved in our study from games to computers to language to psychology to philosophy, we discovered a consistent set of attitudes, beliefs and assumptions that we eventually labeled the "computer mentality." The computer mentality is concerned with computers only to a point; its main business is mind. Its vision of intelligence begins with genetic codes in the primordial soup, continues through the evolutionary development of brains (the extension of which are our present-day primitive computers) and reaches as far as intelligent machines will be able to travel through the galaxies. The computer mentality regards both brains and computers as incidental to the abstract patterns that underlie and activate them.

The issues of artificial intelligence, language, what is human, what is mind are foundational issues. The people working in these areas will shape our lives and our children's lives. Whether we like to admit it or not, they will influence what and how we will think. Already our culture has changed—even Christian culture—and we cannot help being affected by it.

So what began as a family concern has developed into a book about the strange, fascinating world of computers, artificial intelligence, the computer mentality, its language and its metaphors. It is also about humankind and God. We are painfully aware of its shortcomings. Almost every day, it seems, we see a new study published or some new advance in computer research announced that would strengthen or weaken some point; or a colleague asks, "Did you include . . . ?" "Did you talk about . . . ?" "Did you read . . . ?" Nevertheless, we hope that whatever this book does, it will point out some of the issues that will have to be addressed by Christian parents, educators and apologists if we and our children are to have an intellectually responsible, Christian approach to a world where intelligent machines are viewed as human and humans as intelligent machines.

The Challenge of the Computer Mentality

Artificial intelligence is the grand, or perhaps grandiose, enterprise of writing computer programs that can do things that we would consider intelligent if done by human beings—the enterprise of constructing a mind. But there is more. It also contends that the workings of the human mind can be completely explained in the computational language of programs. This enterprise is fast becoming one of the major, if not the foremost, competitors in the age-old endeavor of understanding human nature.

The ideas behind artificial intelligence have a powerful attraction because they can be tested and then accepted or rejected on the basis of experimental evidence. For the technologically oriented mind, these ideas seem to have what it takes to think about mind. Literary, mythological and even biblical imagery, which have hitherto been used to describe the mysterious workings of the mind, are giving way to the new metaphors. The ultimate meanings and referents of these metaphors are lines of code in a computer program. You can say exactly what you mean, point to the code, examine it, manipulate it, transform it and activate it on the computer so that it becomes a dynamic process that almost seems to have life—a mind of its own.

The new terminology for the mind, the new images and metaphors, are being coined in university and military artificial-intelligence laboratories across the world and are fast becoming the new currency for thinking about ourselves. This set of terms is already displacing or transforming conventional psychological language, if only because the computational language seems to explain in a more functional way the older notions of looking at the mind. The idea that mind is a set of programs brings with it its own inherent system of values. Even if Christians look closely at the shiny new coin, they may not recognize what they really see, what the coin really represents.

These ideas are not confined to a scientist's laboratory or a cognitive psychologist's study. We find them in bookstore after bookstore in an array of books aimed at the general market; this category of publishing, according to a recent issue of *Publishers Weekly*, is one of the fastest growing. The ideas turn up in movies and appear in various college courses. They have moved into the elementary classroom. And nothing popularizes abstract ideas faster than their commercial and military applications.

But many people are surprised to hear claims that the mind is a set of programs. How can anyone with a grain of sense entertain such a notion? they wonder. How can we build intelligence out of something so mechanical? What about consciousness, originality, intention, perceptions, imagination and feelings—all those things that make us human and unlike God's other creatures? How could anyone be so deluded when every single moment of daily experience presents such obvious and contrary evidence?

The computer mentality faces these issues and attempts to explain them; in fact, it claims that we are the deluded ones (and probably aren't too bright either). There was a time, it says, when leading Christian thinkers attempted to stamp out the idea that the earth moves around the sun. This so-called heresy threatened humanity's place as the focal point of the universe. Furthermore, the heliocentric theory contradicted the evidence—anyone could look up in the sky and see what went around what. Yet today nobody gets upset about such things; the idea of humanity's uniqueness has managed to survive. People today know that it's not so much the outer universe that makes people special as it is a person's inner universe, the mind. And so here we have drawn our lines of defense—and here is where the computer mentality is laying siege. We are like those medieval church leaders—claims the computer mentality—stuck in our anxiety over our specialness and deluded by what seems to be the irrefutable evidence of our mental experiences.

Nothing Buttery?

For openers, the computer mentality asks us to look at ourselves. Our brains are composed of billions of neurons, not one of which is intelligent, every one of which is an insensate, mechanical, unconscious bit of protoplasm. It's all in how these myriads of neurons are connected to each other and how they act in concert that gives rise to every attribute of the mind. The processes and procedures that these neurons initiate the computer mentality calls *programs,* programs which just happen to run on machines made of flesh and blood instead of silicon and metal. Therefore, humanity is the prime example of how intelligence, feeling, intuition, and the like, can emerge from the interactions of unintelligent components.

At first glance the AI (artificial intelligence) enterprise looks like that old bugaboo, reductionism—"nothing buttery," as brain physiologist and Christian apologist Donald MacKay has put it. The mind is *nothing but* a bunch of computerlike programs. But if we look again, we see that the computer mentality is not so much concerned with reducing everything mental to something metal, as it is in constructing and building wholes from parts.

But this, as we have said, is just for openers. We mention it because there is a tendency for people, Christians in particular, to dismiss the new paradigm out of hand, not realizing that it does attempt to provide answers—though answers written in computer language. This language is taking hold of the imaginations of all kinds of people, not just computer scientists, engineers, mathematicians and physicists. In fact, this is a prime misconception about the computer—that because it is a tool for technical and scientific people, its ideological influence is therefore restricted to that segment of society. But in truth it affects (and sometimes captivates) all who use it: medical doctors, biologists, psychologists, businesspeople, managers, musicians, graphic artists, filmmakers, novelists and, most importantly, schoolchildren.

This raises another misconception: the notion that the computer is a mere tool, a giant calculator and nothing else. But it has, says MIT psychologist and sociologist Sherry Turkle, a second nature. In her six-year study of 200 children and 200 adults of every kind of personality, background and interest, from machine addicts to machine haters, she documents in *The Second Self* the way in which computers have evolved into powerful psychological machines that affect how people think.[2] For children who play with computer toys, use the computer for manipulating information and visual images, or learn to program, Turkle finds that the computer enters into the development of their personalities, their identities and even their sexuality.

A child from four to eight years of age wants to know what this machine is. Is it alive? Does it think? Does it have feelings? Is it different from me? We make a serious error in dismissing young children's reflections about the aliveness or the thinking capabilities of computers as something they will grow out of. A new philosophy of human nature is afoot, and almost every single issue and argument that it raises has already been raised by the children in Turkle's study. The most advanced thinkers and young children wonder about the same deep, philosophical matters, while the rest of us have no idea what is going on. And yet it is important, very important, for us in-betweeners to enter the discussion. We may be the last generation to believe that intelligence, life and consciousness are unified only in the human being. We may be the last to feel outrage, or at least uneasiness, at having them split apart. The next generation may well be the first to believe that human beings are not the only aware intelligences.

More Misconceptions

Another misconception that makes people reject the idea that mind is program is the notion that machines only do what we tell them to do, whereas humans behave in unpredictable, unprogrammed ways. The computer mentality, which is not about to let this go unchallenged, responds in a number of ways. But perhaps the most interesting rebuttal comes not from a computer scientist but from a class of fifth graders that Turkle observed. As the class was discussing whether or not computers are alive, a child asserted that they could not be alive because they are programmed. Everyone thought that a most satisfying answer—except Carla, a quiet girl who seldom went against the crowd. "Well, I don't know if they are alive. They certainly are not completely alive, but I don't think it has to do with that they're programmed. We are all programmed."[3] That answer could have been given by any computer scientist who has a computer mentality.

The computer mentality can make other replies—replies that don't refer the argument back to the human mind and leave the question hanging. For example, we don't have to tell the computer everything it needs to know; we can instruct it how to learn. Programmers can set up evolutionary systems that will leave them so far behind that they have no idea what the computer will do. Line by line a program may be simple and transparent, but at a certain level of complexity its behavior is no longer predictable.

Then, too, new ideas about computer architecture are radically changing the conventional notion of program as it has existed since the advent of the computer—namely, multiprocessing and neural computers. The multiprocessing concept puts many computers, perhaps hundreds, working concurrently on the same problem, each of which may have a different approach or viewpoint, each of which cooperates or perhaps even competes with another. The neural computer is a radically different type of computer, patterned after the way neurons work together in interconnected nets in the brain. Both multiprocessing and neural-net computers provide plenty of surprises for their designers.

This brings up another misconception about computers: computers cannot deal with inexactness or fuzziness. The computer mentality readily acknowledges that any true intelligence must be able to deal with conflicting information and competing goals. An intelligent program is structured to transcend the dilemma when the moment arrives to act. Intelligent programs must be able to deal with the unexpected or the accidental and know how to act in such a situation. Although there are few programs written for conventional computers that can deal satisfactorily with such things, neural computers, in particular, seem to handle conflicting, incomplete and inaccurate information much along the lines that humans do.

There are serious problems with all the arguments cited here. But

we must not let the arguments and counterarguments distract us from
the real issue. Our primary concern should not be whether computers
can or cannot be made to think like people. Rather, the central issue
is how computers are changing our thinking about thought, reality
and ourselves. If we believe that we can dismiss the computer mentality by saying that computers can't do this or that, we will miss its
hold on the imagination. No matter what the future of artificial intelligence, the enterprise is affecting our notions of reason, understanding, intuition, volition, the mind and body, the animate and the in-
animate, consciousness, the self and the soul.

The computer mentality raises forgotten or ignored religious and
philosophical issues with a new urgency. Its vocabulary is filled with
the terms and overtones of philosophy and theology. And its viewpoint is everywhere—from offices to the classrooms to movie theaters.
Its effect will continue whether or not it succeeds in creating a true
intelligence. This is a reason why nontechnical people, people who
think they have no concern with computers, people who love the
humanities and are steeped in the Christian tradition, should enter
the discussion and respond.

The computer enterprise, then, particularly artificial intelligence, is
the beginning of a great adventure, one of the greatest scientific and
technical adventures of all time, ranking in importance with the in-
vention of writing and the printing press—all technologies that shape
the mind. But the issues it raises are complex. We hope to convey the
excitement and frustrations of the enterprise without becoming overly
technical.

In the next chapter we provide an overview of the field, its history
and successes and failures, before introducing some of the people
and ideas we will consider in greater detail in later chapters. The third
chapter compares the brain and the computer. It is fashionable to
explain the brain by using the computer metaphor, which has already
gone a long way toward convincing many of us that we are sophisticated computers—or perhaps not quite so good as a computer. By
comparing how the brain works (or at least how neurophysiologists
think it works) to how the computer works, we can answer some
compelling questions: How does the conventional computer work—

at least in concept? Do the basic switching units in brains, the neurons, behave like the transistors in a computer? Are we faster, slower? Better, worse? This chapter also lays the groundwork for a discussion of how the more brainlike neural computers are constructed and what their capabilities are.

Subsequent chapters will take us into the world of artificial intelligence, provide examples of actual AI programs, let us hear what children and philosophers are saying about the aliveness of the machine, show us how computers affect our intimate relationships, introduce us to the newest and most compelling theories of mind, and make us privy to a radical shift in the definition of humankind. But there may be a few surprises along the way for concerned Christians. We may have to reorient some of our views. We may need to place more importance on issues that we have neglected. We may even need to discard some notions we shouldn't have held to begin with.

We hope you enjoy this journey into a strange and fascinating world.

2
SEARCHING
FOR A SMART
MACHINE

No great idea has a definite starting point. There are always precursors that prepare the way. The same is true with the computer mentality; it has a long history.

Mark the year 1936 as the beginning of the era of computers, information processing and artificial intelligence. And mark Alan Turing, a twenty-four-year-old British mathematician and logician, who published a paper in the *Proceedings of the London Mathematics Society* called "On Computable Numbers, with an Application to the Entscheidungsproblem." Everything about the computer revolution and what it portends—the way it affects our everyday lives and thoughts, the machines, money and hype—began here.

If Turing had said that we were descended from apes, nobody would have missed the implications. But his paper merely sought to prove that certain kinds of mathematical problems cannot be solved by a list of fixed and precise procedures. Indeed, his conclusion in itself doesn't concern us; yet what Turing dreamed up in the process of proving his conjecture does concern us. He needed a way to describe the basic mathematics in its simplest, most primitive terms. Take addition, for example: move from one column of figures to the next, write or change a particular number, and organize all the individual actions into a fixed procedure that guarantees the correct answer every time. What are some of the basics? Move from one location to another and write a figure.

Turing conjured up an imaginary machine that could perform these simple operations. He pictured a device with an infinitely long tape partitioned into squares, similar to toilet paper. The machine had a marker to indicate which square the machine was scanning at any moment. Each square could contain only one symbol—either a "1" or a "0"—or it could be blank. All Turing needed were ones and zeros to represent numbers and words, just as the dots and dashes of Morse code do. The string of ones and zeros on the tape represented the input, and then the "given" data was manipulated by the machine into another string of ones and zeros, which represented the desired answer, the output.

Anything that a modern computer can do today—from figuring payroll to controlling a worldwide weapons system, from proving mathematical theorems to diagnosing diseases or serving as a therapist—is reducible to a list of commands similar to those above. Everything a conventional digital computer has done, or ever will do, can be accomplished with a Turing machine. Moreover, the Turing machine defines quite clearly the organizing concept behind what Alvin Toffler calls the *third wave*. That concept of "information processing" (of which information *theory* is the larger context) is merely the idea of moving and changing a sequence of individual symbols one at a time, according to a list of instructions.

The Turing machine is a mathematical system—not a real machine as its name would suggest—and Turing did not invent the computer as we know it today. But he opened the field of artificial intelligence. This fact in itself is significant since it anticipates a curious hallmark of the AI enterprise: AI is not about machines at all. We must always keep this fact in mind. In theory it matters little whether the machine that manipulates the symbols is a clattering paper-tape contraption, a powerful modern computer or the human brain itself. AI researchers want all the efficiency and power they can get to run their programs, but the machine itself is unimportant.

In the decade after Turing's paper, vacuum-tube computers were built along the lines of his paper-and-pencil model. The instructions were carried out by humans working with electromechanical switches and, later on, plugboards. To make the machine carry out its instructions, the operator had to throw the switches in the correct order or plug the wires into the plugboard in the right configuration (like a telephone operator at a switchboard). The data, encoded as strings of ones and zeros on the outside, took their internal electronic form as on or off tubes.

The primary characteristic of early computers was that each new problem required the operator to rewire the machine. Mathematician John von Neumann conceived the idea of storing the list of instructions inside the machine in exactly the same way that the data were stored—as strings of ones and zeros. Once the instructions and data were loaded into the machine, no one would need to physically rewire the machine for each new task. Once activated, electrical circuits initiate the first instruction, which in turn opens certain switches and closes others that do their part to translate the data into the required form. In serial fashion, the process continues until all the instructions have been exhausted. Although today's transistors have replaced vacuum tubes as the basic switching units, the basic design of all conventional computers has remained exactly as von Neumann first conceived it.

But we are not through with Alan Turing. In 1947 Turing wrote "Intelligent Machinery," which was not published until 1969, fifteen years after his death. In this paper he outlined his ideas concerning the possibility of intelligent machines, using the analogy of man and machine as his guiding principle. He reasoned that intelligent machines were a possibility, since brains are machines and they certainly can think. There are machines, he argued, that already imitate the various parts of the human being: the television camera is the eye;

the microphone is the ear; robotic servomechanisms imitate arms and hands—and then he got to the brain.

The Turing Test

Turing thought that we could produce fairly accurate electrical models to copy the way nerves work. The electrical circuits used in computers already have all the essential properties of nerves—both transmit information from place to place and store it. Why couldn't a machine be taught along the same lines that we teach children? It could be disciplined with a system of rewards and punishments, given initiative and at a certain point be allowed to make its own decisions.

Some of Turing's ideas remain in the center of the AI enterprise, while others have fallen into disrepute. There are arguments and counterarguments to Turing's man-machine analogy, some of which we will examine later. But one all-important concern surfaces immediately: What does it mean to say that a machine can think?

Turing turned to this question in his 1950 paper "Computing Machinery and Intelligence."[1] He stated that we must go beyond our standard uses for "machines" and "thinking"; everyone can come up with different meanings, and around and around we go. He proposed replacing the original question with another—closely related but unambiguous. By asking both a machine and a human a series of questions and then listening carefully to their replies, the question "Can a machine think?" becomes "Can you tell the difference between the machine's responses and the person's?" If you can't, the machine thinks and is intelligent. Turing called this the "imitation game," though everyone today refers to it as merely the "Turing Test."

Turing predicted that by the year 2000 a machine would pass his test, but nobody, not even the staunchest AI supporter, is so optimistic. Indeed, it would seem as though we could always fashion questions that would expose a machine as an intellectual fraud. For example, how would a computer respond to questions involving poetry or music, anything that concerns sensibility, anything that stands on the boundary of thought and feeling? Moreover, would it be able to tell the difference between itself and a human?

Many people who resent the idea that machines might ever think believe that questions about poetry, feeling and so forth dispose of the AI enterprise. That is a serious mistake. A machine could fail the Turing Test and still be considered intelligent—just distinguishable from a human.

Thoughts versus Behavior

So what are we to make of the Turing Test? Despite its apparent objectivity, does it really take us anywhere? Is it really so important after all? We can see where it has led and what form it has taken by looking at the accepted definition of artificial intelligence: the science of making machines do things that would require intelligence if done by humans. Notice that the issue of whether a machine can think is missing, just as Turing had hoped. Notice, too, the change in perspective: instead of determining what intelligence is and then asking if machines are capable of it, we now have "intelligence is what intelligence does." Again, this was Turing's main point. Or we can put it another way, the way Claude Shannon, working for Bell Labs in the 1940s, put it. Processing information, what scientists believe intelligence does, has nothing to do with meaning, but with manipulation. It doesn't matter whether the thing processing information has intelligence—understands what it does—so long as the results, the information processed, appear intelligent. This is crucial to understanding what computer researchers and cognitive psychologists intend when they talk about intelligence, human or otherwise. Content or meaning is unimportant; what counts is manipulating symbols, whether letters, numbers or ideas. The 1940s was a time of great intellectual ferment on this whole notion of information. We are only now beginning to see the tangible results of the thinking of such men as Turing, Shannon and von Neumann.

Behind the whole intelligence debate lurks an ominous assumption: it doesn't matter if a machine ever passes the Turing Test; the real issue is not whether machines can think, but whether we think they do and, conversely, whether we think like machines. In other words, what do we understand about ourselves and how we think? Do we explain our thinking with computer metaphors? Do we understand the brain as nothing more than a computer, a program? We have a natural tendency to turn things around, almost as if we were subject to some kind of powerful linguistic force field. If we hear often enough that we are machines, a mere analogy, we will come to believe it reflects the literal truth: the faulty metaphor has become reality. By creating a machine that embodies our essential nature, humanity re-creates itself in its own eyes, in its own mind and in its own image. We shall see how powerful and how well-developed the AI model of mind as program has become.

The underlying thinking and the intention behind the Turing Test are very much with us. In important matters, Turing was eminently successful. After discrediting the question "Can machines think?" as too meaningless to deserve discussion, he wrote: "Nevertheless I believe that at the end of the century the use of words and general educated opinion will have altered so much that one will be able to speak of machines thinking without expecting to be contradicted."[2] This prediction is right on target. The idea of a thinking machine is being absorbed into our language and opinions without our ever asking, Is this possible? Words and the way we use them are the key. Although the notion of a thinking machine cannot completely happen without a major shift in the way we think of ourselves and the way we view reality, the shift is already occurring.

Constructing Intelligence

We have seen the beginnings of both computers and artificial intelligence in the work of Alan Turing. Yet what most of us know about computers seems far removed from Turing and his hypothetical machine—at least so far as the development of the computer itself is concerned.

Everyone knows that computers are becoming more powerful and speedier or that they are becoming easier to use. Just about everyone has had some dealings with a computer and probably works with one on the job. News about computers is everywhere. Everyone has heard about programs and software—put these disks in your machine and your management, communications, inventory and personal-finance problems are solved.

Yet artificial intelligence is still not a common term, though we are hearing more about smart machines or intelligent software. But since artificial intelligence is the force behind a new thrust in business and economics, as well as a new definition of humanity, we should have some idea of where it has been in the past three decades since Alan Turing and where it is today.

In the early years—the late fifties and sixties—AI researchers toyed with games like checkers and chess. To the researchers, this seemed like the most reasonable area to begin constructing intelligence for two reasons. First, the style of thinking that games and mathematics require was naturally attractive to them. Second, games are the easiest kinds of situations to program. A game is closed from the world; its actions are few and simple. Compared with all the hum and buzz of real life, a game is clear-cut and ready-made for computer logic.

One of the first efforts to construct a program that might be truly intelligent was begun in the late 1940s by Arthur Samuel, who was then employed at IBM. He based his program on the way neurons work in the human brain, and he equipped it with a system of rewards and punishments. His program would play checkers with human opponents and improve its play by modifying its internal structure according to whether it won or lost. It was, and is, one of the outstanding examples of a machine that can learn from its mistakes. After hundreds of games, the program gradually improved; it could beat its creator. After more than three decades of playing and learning, it is now capable of beating amateurs and can defeat all but the best tournament players. Unfortunately, the principles behind Samuel's program could not be extended to other areas of AI research (for basic mathematical reasons), and AI investigators soon abandoned the approach despite its promise. This would be a footnote in AI history were it not that intense research has begun again on programs that resemble the brain. Researchers think that they have overcome the problems inherent in Samuel's work and have seen impressive results—and not with checkers.

Nevertheless, research proceeded along the lines of discovering what rules humans use in solving problems and then mechanizing them. AI researchers have separated their rules into two main groups: algorithms and heuristics. We encountered algorithms when we discussed the Turing machine: a specific list of steps that guarantees the right answer every time. A heuristic, on the other hand, is merely a rule of thumb, guaranteeing nothing: for example, "The best defense is a good offense," "The early bird gets the worm" and "When in doubt, drop back and punt." At times, heuristics seem like proverbs or maxims. Indeed, they embody judgment, experience and wisdom; they attempt to point the way. Heuristic thinking is what we need to play more complicated games. Such simple games as tic-tac-toe can be won or drawn by using algorithms only. But try to approach chess this way, knowing exactly what will happen under certain conditions and plotting your course to the end of the game. It would take the fastest computer in existence the entire age of the universe to complete a single game. You need to reduce the possibilities, the predictions, by using heuristic strategies. On the average, even the best human players look ahead only two or three plays.

The search for heuristics, the strategies we use in problem solving, was an important direction for AI in its early years. It remains so today. Almost immediately the field began to broaden from games to other sorts of problem-solving activities commonly found in mathematics, logic and ordinary puzzles. AI soon lost any preoccupation it might have had with machines and entered the field of psychology.

Rather than rely on mathematical logic, an AI researcher would interview an expert to mine those nuggets of wisdom that make him or her so proficient and then code them for the computer. Today we call such programs expert systems. To a degree, this approach has been successful: twenty years ago there were chess programs that could defeat better-than-average players; today a person must be at the master level to trounce most state-of-the-art programs. To reach this point computers have relied more and more on brute force, that is, increased memory capacity or mechanical power brought about by technology rather than superior heuristics or intelligence.

Nevertheless, certain kinds of programs exist that exhibit what we would call intelligence or at least certain aspects of intelligence, if we were talking about people. These programs diagnose medical problems, plan molecular genetic experiments, analyze mass spectrographs and infer protein structures from electric density maps—to name a few. These expert systems use a tremendous amount of detailed and painstakingly garnered information and, in some cases, outperform their human counterparts. They have the ability to make complex logical inferences by extensive use of heuristics, which gives them flexibility and some measure of ingenuity.

These programs can change and adapt, grow in knowledge and learn. They can also be unpredictable; more comes out of them than their designers thought went into them. It seems remarkable that machines, programmed in advance, fundamentally reducible to the primitive left-right-type operations of the Turing machine, could produce anything really surprising. Yet they do. For example, programs capable of proving theorems in logic and mathematics have discovered ideas that were completely unknown to their designers. But all these expert systems have a serious drawback when it comes to extending their prowess beyond their severely limited domains. Genuine intelligence must be adaptable from one situation to the next. Certainly we don't require that women and men be experts in all fields, but we do expect some principles to carry over from one situation to another—the ability to ask penetrating questions, for instance, or to make interesting comparisons and analogies. These are things computers cannot yet accomplish.

Intelligence is more than the ability to prove certain theorems or play championship chess. It involves understanding ordinary language, learning through mistakes, applying principles from one set of circumstances to another, the ability to make abstractions. It took years for AI researchers to come to this conclusion, but suddenly ordinary intelligence—what we might call common sense—took on a new luster. Even the human propensity to make mistakes, to forget, to tolerate sloppiness, to live with inconsistencies, to form unscientific beliefs, to create stereotypes and to make sweeping generalizations about everything and anything were looked at in a new light. Researchers had considered all these things characteristic of a lack of intelligence. Then they thought that perhaps they are *essential* to the functioning of genuine intelligence. Perhaps without them, negative though they might be, human beings could not survive, let alone act rationally.

Consider forgetting, for example. If each bit of information that our minds need to get through a single day were all equally clear and present to us, we would never make it to the breakfast table and that first cup of coffee. It would be total mental overload. Because we can forget, our brains are saved from being helplessly clogged. Could any human relationships survive without forgetting? Could we ever forgive each other? Could we ever forgive ourselves? Could we ever emulate the woman caught in adultery by obeying Jesus' command to go and sin no more? Forgive and forget—these are two different yet inextricably intertwined commands. Often it seems that we need to forget the trivial to remember what is really important. In this respect we reflect the image of God: he forgets our heedless acts, our sins and our shortcomings, and remembers our words of confession and our pleas for grace.

The nature of memory keenly interests AI researchers. At some point, if they succeed, the old adage about learning from mistakes · will apply to both machines and people. As humans, we store in our brains the contextual information surrounding our errors so that the next time a similar circumstance arises, we will have learned something from the past. From then on our mental associations are altered, and our reality is never again the same. This is the kind of memory and the kind of learning that researchers are endeavoring to give their programs—along with a sense of anticipation. When circumstances don't turn out as expected, these programs would dynamically alter the structure of their memories to create a new set of anticipations.

The real test for AI, however, is to understand ordinary language. Some three decades ago there was a great deal of interest in the machine translation of texts from one language into another. Researchers used a dictionary-grammar approach: a computer would match the dictionary definitions of a word in both languages, then separate the sentences into subject, predicate, object, indirect object and so forth. Modern linguists have shown that this is not the way humans understand language. The classic example, now part of AI folklore, is the computer rendition of Jesus' famous observation in the Garden of Gethsemane, "The spirit is willing, but the flesh is weak," into the Russian sentence "The vodka is strong, but the meat is rotten."

Today machine translation is on the back burner of AI research; this is not true of the study of language, which is central to information theory as well as information processing. The modern approach is not to start with a finished language, as in translation, but to build it from basic components—to develop some kind of serviceable language from scratch even if it lacks the complexity or richness of a natural language.

Even so, today you can buy a machine you can talk to. Your conversation would have to be limited to what the machine knows, but if you did so limit yourself, it would understand you and respond intelligently. (And here, again, we come to the crux of the matter. We use the words *understand* and *respond intelligently* because we have no other words to describe the machine's behavior without resorting to the technical language of programming. We feel compelled to talk about the computer as if it were a human being, even though AI researchers themselves readily concede that programs can't understand ordinary language as can a human being—though in the computer field "can't" is always followed by "yet.")

The machine can translate the sound of your voice into symbolic patterns, identify individual words and phrases, analyze their syntax, contextualize them in their memory, make thousands of logical inferences from them and then respond in your native tongue. If you based your judgment on behavior alone, you would say it was human. Without thinking, we accept the criteria behind the Turing Test and find that the machine hasn't done too badly. Yet it *understands* nothing. The program has merely manipulated symbols like a fancy typewriter, a capability provided by a human programmer, while the person speaking to it has provided all the interpretation and understanding. Or so it would seem.

Here is a machine that listens, reasons and communicates. AI claims that understanding does not lie in the biological brain alone but in relationships; therefore we can find understanding somewhere between us and the Turing machine. Yet between "left-right-type" and a Shakespearean sonnet there is a barrier of complexity that researchers are trying to penetrate. They look for programs that can manipulate other programs in ever-increasing layers of complexity, some groups of programs organized in hierarchies, some in thousands of democracies—cooperating one moment, competing the next. At a certain level of complexity, the barrier is overcome. Intelligence emerges. This is the theoretical basis for AI's vision, not that AI research knows how to accomplish all this.

What evidence is there that would allow us to believe that intelligence may come out of an unintelligent system of chips and codes? AI's answer is quick and sure: our own brains are just one example of such a system. Yet there is a difference, despite the behavioral criteria. People are conscious of their actions and words. Programs are not. AI researchers claim that consciousness will emerge from the myriads of interactions between programs, just as intelligence will. Besides, they ask, what is the connection between intelligence and consciousness anyway? Poets, artists and scientists alike say that they do their most imaginative work when they are not conscious of what they do. So, again, we are left with saying that programs understand—and yet they don't. They are not conscious of what they do; yet we are likewise unconscious of the vast majority of the brain's activities.

The Shape of Things to Come

But this is just a brief introduction to the enterprise of artificial intelligence, where it started and what it has done. Despite its failures, it is astounding that researchers have made a contrivance that can reason at any level. But let's take a quick look at the future.

In a few years, we won't be dealing with handfuls of smart machines costing hundreds of thousands of dollars, but with interactive networks that in comparison will cost loose change. These machines in a matter of minutes or seconds will continuously update each other with technical and common-sense knowledge that took years to garner. Add to this the people who will be working with these machines: thousands of natural intelligences hooked up with thousands of artificial ones—talking, teaching, learning, discovering, working on the same problems at the same time; being monitored, directed and organized by the most intimate amalgam of people and technology that the world has ever known. Every corner of our lives will be filled with an alien blend of both kinds of intelligence, and it will become increasingly difficult to tell which is which.

Most of the technology is already here—it is simply a matter of hooking us all up. And that is happening right now in elementary schools, universities, the military and business. The next generations won't feel and respond to this new situation as we do now; they will have been assimilated. This is important to remember. We too easily become caught up in arguments about the failures and accomplishments of computers and artificial intelligence and overlook the thing that should concern us most—how our view of humanity, how we think about ourselves, will be affected.

We are talking about theological issues, not about lifestyle changes or how the marketplace will look. If you can't tell a machine from a person in the way it talks and acts (appearance doesn't count), or if your mind-set does not allow for such distinctions, how do we proceed with a definition of human nature that includes something so unprovable as a soul? Too often we Christians fail to realize the extent to which our thinking is formed by our culture, particularly when it comes to our emphasis on rationality and reason. (For example, do we ever stop to think how fully we've absorbed Freud's notions, or Darwin's, despite protestations to the contrary?) We're not just talking about our theorem-proving, game-playing, analytic powers, which the computer is already capable of emulating. We cannot take refuge in saying that artificial intelligence doesn't try to get at the deepest level of what we mean by reason, because that is precisely what it is after. And if AI cannot produce it on a machine for another century or two, it will, nevertheless, provide the most attractive and acceptable explanation of mind around.

We have identified too closely with the tenets and ideas of humanism—particularly the notion that when we speak of mind and rationality, we are speaking of soul, and vice versa. But this book is not a polemic against rationality, or AI, for that matter. Our quarrel is with the computer mentality. We will point out some of AI's problems and shortcomings, but we will not attempt to prove its impossibility. We think that as a science it may have much to teach us and, as such, is not anti-Christian any more than is physics or biology. Christians can share in the AI enterprise and, indeed, will have no other choice if it is our intention to be educated and do business in the world.

3
THE COMPUTER
AND THE
BRAIN

When people speak of the computer, they are referring to the digital computer, the only kind that has been widely available for the past three decades or so. The design of a digital computer is different from that of the human brain, and this difference shows up quite clearly in the type of problem solving each does best. If you need to make extensive calculations or logical inferences with millions of pieces of information, it is best to use a computer. On the other hand, if you want to recognize the face of an old school chum at a reunion, you would be wise to trust your own brain; a digital computer would be useless.

Recently, however, a radically new type of computer has made its appearance, a computer fashioned after the brain. Even at this early stage of development, it has the ability to recognize patterns, such as handwriting or faces, which the digital computer finds extremely difficult or even impossible. But this is the merest hint of the difference between the digital computer and the new brainlike machine, called the neural computer (or neural network). People have said that computers can never approach human intelligence even in theory because everything must be programmed for them; therefore, they can never learn anything on their own or deal with the unexpected (though some AI researchers would take issue with this even for digital computers). However, neural computers do not run the same kinds of programs as digital computers. In fact, they are not so much programmed as they are *trained*, somewhat in the way we humans learn. Because they are modeled after the brain, not only can they do things that are practically impossible for digital computers, they also have difficulty with the same activities we do, such as performing long computations quickly and accurately.

Let's assume that all we know about a digital computer is that we can store words and numbers in it electronically and manipulate them through a list of instructions called a program. Before we can appreciate how digital computers differ from brains or neural computers, we need to answer two basic questions: How do words and numbers look in the machine? How is it possible to do anything with them?

Words and Numbers Machine-Style

We have just typed the word CAT on our computer keyboard. If we lift the cover from the computer, we would not see the letters C-A-T anywhere in its hardware—no more than we would expect to find them printed on the surface of our brains after reading them. But we can use the fact that electricity is either *on* or *off* to create a code that represents words and numbers in the machine—something like a Morse code of *offs* and *ons* instead of dots and dashes. Although different manufacturers use different codes, here is CAT in one of them:

C: on-off-off-off-off-on-on
A: on-off-off-off-off-off-on
T: on-off-on-off-on-off-off

Inside the computer are rows of tiny devices called transistors that can be turned on or off to give us the coded configuration for CAT. The closest we can come to actually seeing what CAT looks like in the computer is to have it type out the state of each particular transistor, called a bit, by using 1 for on and 0 for off. So here is CAT in machine code: 1000011 1000001 1010100. In like fashion all words and numbers are represented inside the computer by strings of on/off bits and appear on the outside in their most primitive form in machine code as strings of 0s and 1s.

Most of us are aware that the much-advertised computer revolution has something to do with Silicon Valley and semiconductors—the connection being that silicon is the basic material of most transistors. Silicon in its natural state is a poor conductor of electricity. But if we dope a silicon crystal with a carefully controlled amount of phosphorus, it will conduct a small negative charge. If we dope it with boron, it becomes capable of conducting a small positive charge. Either way, coated silicon becomes a semiconductor, a material that conducts electricity under one set of circumstances but not under others. Transistors are composed of each type of semiconductor, along with silicon dioxide (glass) for insulation and aluminum strips for conducting electricity. "Cheap and small" has been the key to the enormous commercial success of computers. For pennies, hundreds of thousands of transistors can be printed on a chip smaller than a fourth of a thumbnail.

On/off pulses give us more than just a means of coding words and numbers; they can also mean yes/no, right/wrong or true/false. They enable us to stand apart from our data and make decisions about it. This is the first step in giving the machine reasoning power, but we need something more if we want to put words and numbers together in logical patterns. That "something more," the most powerful concept in the computer world, is NOT. Using two different transistors, we can build an "inverter," the mechanical version of NOT, which changes *off* to *on* or *on* to *off*, thus giving us the power to change any word or number, bit by bit. It also gives us the ability to change our decisions; what was false in one circumstance can become true in another or vice versa.

The inverter, NOT, is the beginning of mechanized thought. It is but a small step to build AND and OR, giving us all we need to construct the grammar of logic. Once we have NOT and OR, we can build IF THEN, one of the most important and useful devices in constructing artificial intelligence. Furthermore, using two NOTs, three ANDs and an OR, we can build a simple adding machine, and from here we can develop subtraction, multiplication, division and all the complex mathematical operations that a computer can perform. Although a digital computer is a complicated machine, all that it can do with words, numbers, logic, language and mathematics arises from thousands and thousands of combinations of a few basic devices, each of which reduces to NOTs wired in various series or parallel circuits.

We now have an idea how transistors make NOTs, ANDs and ORs, which in turn make possible almost every function of the digital computer. Next we need to know how to communicate with the machine and how the machine does what we tell it to do.

Talking to Machines

There are approximately one hundred basic operations wired into the computer, each one consisting of various combinations of NOTs, ANDs and ORs, or their equivalents. Each of these fundamental operations—for example, adding, storing, fetching or branching after making a comparison—is itself identified by a unique string of 0s and 1s. When we want the computer to do something with the encoded words and numbers we have previously stored in it, we instruct it by selecting and ordering some of these basic operations. The result is a program. If we write our program by typing in the unique string of 0s and 1s for each operation, we are programming in what is known as machine language, the most direct and elemental way to communicate with the machine.

But people find machine language difficult, time-consuming and tedious. To get around this we throw in a few letters, such as ADD or STO (store), to take the place of some of the 0s and 1s. Now we have assembly language. It is relatively easy for an assembler program to then translate this assembly language into the pure 0s and 1s of machine language, pretty much a one-to-one translation of groups of letters into their corresponding strings of bits. This helps us, but not much. So we invent such higher level languages as BASIC, FOR-

TRAN, PASCAL, COBOL or LISP to make life easier.

We've all seen rows of books in our local bookstores with some of these names in the titles. These languages comprise individual words, phrases and mathematical notations that, though they may look incomprehensible, are a lot closer to our natural language than machine or assembly language. Their rigid, limited, grammatical and syntactical structures are translated into assembly language and then into machine language by programs already stored in the computer—a great relief to programmers.

But how does a digital computer actually accomplish inside what the program from the outside tells it to do? One of the breakthrough concepts in the earliest days of computer design was that 0s and 1s can do double duty: not only can they represent actual data, they can also represent the instructions that manipulate the data. Even though both data and instructions are strings of 0s or 1s, the machine uses them based on location—data is stored in one place in the machine, instructions in another. Each unit of information, no matter whether a piece of data or an instruction, must have an address in order for the machine to keep track of what's where—just as the postman needs to know our individual mailbox numbers. Programmers assign these addresses themselves, or the machine's translation programs do it for them. We will see that addressing accounts for one of the most significant differences between the way memory works in digital computers and the way it works in either brains or neural computers.

The programmer usually enters a program through a keyboard. Each instruction is then stored in a special area in the machine. Internal programs translate each instruction into one or more of the hundred or so machine-language operations. Internal circuits fetch the first machine-language instruction and decode it; then through a combination of circuitry and internal programs, the machine goes to the addresses of any data it needs, sends the data to a special working area and operates on it. The machine then fetches the next instruction and operates on it, and so on.

This is crucial to remember: digital computers do things serially, one instruction after another—fetch, execute, fetch, execute—millions or even billions of times a second. They can't accomplish two or more things at once the way humans can—for example, driving a car, reading road signs and talking to our companions; at least they can't the way they are currently designed. But one of the most exciting research developments in digital computer architecture—parallel processing—would help redress this shortcoming. Designers want to hook together several computers, maybe hundreds or even thousands, in some way to enable them to work on one or more problems simultaneously. Such a configuration of computers would begin to function more humanly. Parallel-processing machines already exist, but no one has a good idea how to program them in such a way as to take advantage of their potential. Although some experts predict this will be done in a decade or so, others are skeptical.

The Brain

People are always comparing the computer and the brain; metaphors bounce back and forth like balls in a tennis match. It's natural to want to compare the two in terms of size, strength and quickness. But a more apt comparison would be between an automobile and a horse. Put them on a paved straightaway, and there is no question as to which goes faster; nor is there any doubt which will do better over a narrow path through the deep woods. While the brain processes information, we would not be correct in thinking of it as a kind of digital computer; each has an altogether different design and works on quite different principles.

People who work with or write about the brain almost always use such words as "amazing," "incredible" or "awesome." Some write that it is the most intricate, complicated cubic half-foot in the universe. Others contend that it is a whole universe in itself. How complex is the brain? Consider the number of its cells—ten billion being a conservative estimate. Most of us have become insensitive to the magnitude of such a figure, if only because of the size of the national debt. We would appreciate how many cells or neurons lie in the brain if we had to count each one. Working from nine to five and giving ourselves a second to count each neuron, it would take over a thousand years to do the job.

Counting individual neurons is only a start to comprehending what's inside our heads. A single neuron can connect with anywhere from a few to more than 200,000 other neurons. Scientists estimate that on average a single neuron has roughly 10,000 connections. If we tried to count these neuronal connections under the same working conditions as before, it would take millions of years.

A digital computer has about ten million basic processing elements, each of which is connected to a handful of other elements. This means that the human brain is millions of times more complex than a computer (though many computer designers think that computers eventually will pull even with the brain through parallel processing or by replacing semiconductor technology with something completely different, such as optics).

But merely comparing the numbers of processing elements in computers and brains gives no indication how each is organized. If we look at an enlarged photograph of a computer circuit board, we can't help being impressed with the sheer beauty of its geometrical patterns, the orders within orders and the complexities within complexities. Enhanced by color and given a good frame, such a photo makes a stunning wall hanging. But a blowup of the nerve connections from a piece of stained brain tissue gives quite a different picture. We see an incredibly dense, tangled forest—a chaotic, incomprehensible wasteland, the stuff of nightmares. If we felt compelled to straighten out all the nerve fibers in a brain and lay them neatly end to end, the line would extend well over a 100,000 thousand miles, almost to the moon.

After looking at brains and computers this way, we should not be surprised that people make mistakes and computers don't. That people can do anything at all, much less with reasonable accuracy, is the real surprise. Yet out of all the brain's messy entanglements comes a feature that a conventional computer doesn't share—robustness. At least 10,000 neurons die each day, never to be replaced; yet the brain of an older person works well, if not better than when it was much younger. But if we remove a comparable number of transistors in a computer, or even a handful, the machine simply won't work. The computer is spare, economical and sensitive, whereas the brain is redundant, profligate and tough.

The most obvious difference between digital computers and brains is that we don't program brains by feeding them a list of instructions. Children don't learn to understand or speak their native language by memorizing a list of grammatical rules, nor do they recognize their parents' faces by memorizing lists of formulas specifying all their geometrical features in all positions. So what do brains do differently from computers?

No one knows the entire answer, because no one knows exactly how the brain works. Part of the answer is that the computer's transistors and the brain's neurons are connected differently. Two transistors are joined together by a continuous aluminum strip so that there is a direct, unbroken path to carry the signals. But neurons are not connected directly to other neurons. A tiny gap, called the synapse, separates a conducting nerve fiber of one neuron from another. Signals from a sending neuron are transmitted along a nerve fiber as bursts of tiny, effervescent spikes of voltage that are transformed and carried across the synaptic gap by chemical action and then are transformed back into an electrical effect for the receiving neuron—if the message is to go any farther. The chemical mechanism in the synaptic gap enables a receiving neuron to alter incoming signals by increasing or decreasing their strength before relaying them or even by blocking them completely. Furthermore, a neuron will not relay a series of impulses unless the voltage in its interior reaches a certain level, its *threshold*.

The synaptic gap, along with all the electrochemical actions that occur there, seems to be the most fundamental processing mechanism in the brain. Although far more complicated, it is comparable in importance to the NOT inverter in the computer. Because of its importance, we need to look closer at how it works and how it relates to the neuron.

At the end of a conducting nerve fiber a "button" forms the sending side of the synaptic gap, which contains a large number of tiny spheres, or vesicles, each of which contains several thousand molecules of a chemical called a neurotransmitter. Although there are dozens of known or suspected neurotransmitters, each with different properties, a button contains only one type. When a succession of voltages travels down the nerve and terminates at the button, the vesicles bind to the wall and empty their contents into the fluid in the synaptic gap. In less than half a thousandth of a second, the neurotransmitter molecules travel a millionth of an inch across the gap to a reception site on the target side. Here they bind with special receptor molecules, like so many chemical keys fitting into chemical locks, and thereby either excite or inhibit the target neuron.

If the neurotransmitter is excitatory, it causes the walls of the membrane on the receiving side of the gap to open to a rapid exchange of charged sodium, chloride and potassium atoms that temporarily render the voltage in the interior of the receptor more positive. This small positive charge is immediately distributed throughout the body of the target neuron and will last about 15 thousandths of a second. If the target neuron receives enough positive voltage from different synapses in overlapping time intervals, or if it receives enough repeated charges from the same synapse before they die away, it will reach its threshold and fire off its own burst of voltages to other neurons where the same process will repeat. Even the relative locations of the synapses are a factor. Synapses that lie on or near the body of a neuron are far more excitable than those that lie farther away on more distant nerve fibers. Since ten to twenty per cent of a neuron's synapses lie on its body, space as well as time helps determine whether a neuron reaches its threshold.

But a target neuron does not forward all of the incoming signals it receives, meaning that a great number of its synapses prevent it from reaching its threshold. If our brains worked on an excitatory basis only, we would be a twitching, convulsed mass of protoplasm incapable of thought or action. When an inhibitory neurotransmitter is sent across the synaptic gap, the net effect on the target area is to render its interior voltage more negative, so that even more excitatory impulses than before are required to raise the interior voltage to the threshold.

So each neuron is like a tiny biological computer. It adds the hundreds and thousands of plus and minus voltages bombarding it at any instant, the effects of which overlap both in time and space. Some of these raise the voltage in the body of a target neuron and some lower it—the result being a fluctuating state of a neuron's read-iness to fire, like water rising and falling in a glass until it should happen to reach the top, or threshold, and overflow. Instead of a transistor's all-or-nothing state at any moment, a neuron can be any-where in between.

Neurons, Memory and Change

How do neurons and synapses make learning and memory possible? The answer to this question is fundamental in understanding neural computers. For almost four decades brain scientists thought that neu-rons are connected in distinct groups or assemblies that might over-lap. Some assemblies may be genetically specialized for hearing, vi-sion, smell and so on. In our earliest months and years of development, each of these basic functional assemblies, what some scientists call the "primary repertoire," is established. Because each primary circuit is selective, it will respond only to those signals it is structured to recognize, such as those from the eye but not those from the ear. When a circuit is activated, its synapses are strengthened so that connected neurons can more efficiently stimulate each other.

Not only do neurons within an assembly excite each other, but the assemblies themselves can excite other assemblies, which then arouse others, and so forth. Some brain theorists think that certain assem-blies can *only* be excited by other assemblies, so that what activates them is not external sensory signals but the internal activity of other circuits. It is rather like upper-level managers in a large business who respond only to middle managers and have nothing to do with the factory workers. In this way patterns build on patterns, each level becoming less specific and more inclusive. This gives the brain its great powers of generalization and abstraction.

When the brain is presented with the signals arising from a new experience, a closed loop of neurons fires off just long enough for the brain's perceptual systems to act on it. If we are to remember anything more than momentarily, however, there must be a change in the strength and responsiveness of the synapses in the assembly, a sort of deepening of the grooves. There is mounting evidence that experience causes structural changes in neurons; not only do individual neurons change shape, but the number of synaptic connections between them increases. Moreover, an experience sets up particular sequences of impulses in neuronal circuits that can alter the synaptic strengths, subsequently causing behavioral changes. Because experience can alter the chemical make-up and functioning of a set of neurons in a fixed circuit, brain scientists—and the designers of neural computers—believe this to be the neuronal basis for memory and learning.[1]

This mutability is an obvious difference between the brain and the conventional computer, but we cannot miss another, even more obvious difference: one is wet and one is dry. There are fluids in the brain containing chemicals, such as hormones and neuropeptides, that not only modulate its behavior but actually change its physical make-up. Some of these chemicals affect the excitatory or inhibitory levels in a neuron apart from the effect of the normal neurotransmitters in its synaptic gaps; others bring about long-term changes in a neuron's membrane wall that affect the strength of the synapse or cause the formation of more receptor molecules. As neurophysiologist John Sinclair writes:

> The brain differs from a computer in that it is immersed in a fluid containing many substances that alter the way the system works. The brain is practically a different machine when certain hormones or modulating substances are floating by it, or when we cause some drug to be dissolved in the solution. Substances diffusing around the brain or in local regions of it seem to form a second means of communication, superimposed on the system of neurons and synapses.[2]

Comparisons

Now that we have outlined and contrasted the basic mechanisms of digital computers and brains, we are in a position to make more general comparisons. The means of communication within a digital computer is a code; with the brain, it is a burst of signals. A code represents a message; it conveys meaning in a pattern of on/off impulses that stand for words, numbers or instructions whose significance is imposed from without. Computer code has nothing to do with frequency: only the on/off pattern matters. Whether it takes a billionth of a second to transmit or a thousand years, its significance would not change. So computer code carries a lot of conceptual baggage when it enters the machine, baggage that must be packed by human intelligence. On the other hand, all that brain signals say is, *I'm here, I'm here, I'm here.* It's up to the brain's internal structures to make something of them. The only structure inherent in brain signals is their frequency—how many occur in a given period of time. This affects the accumulation of voltage in the body of a neuron, which in turn affects its readiness to fire.

The digital computer, then, is a thoroughgoing symbol machine, and all its operations are controlled by a single, central processing unit. The brain, however, seems to have no such all-powerful control center that pushes around symbols; indeed, there may not be symbols as such in the brain at all—just neurons acting on neurons in lawful, interacting patterns.

The circuitry of a conventional computer is fixed in metal and silicon; we wouldn't want its innards to grow or diminish or make new connections on its own—not, that is, if we intend to control it with a program. When we send an instruction via a particular sequence of impulses along a given circuit, we expect the same result every time. We cannot suffer our computer's transistors to be affected by internal use or by its environment. None of this holds for the brain or a neural computer. When a memory circuit is created, the connecting synapses are altered, becoming more sensitive to a certain spatio-temporal pattern of impulses. Herein we see how a memory might change over time, become more elaborate or, perhaps, less precise. As life goes on, the strengths of the synaptic connections are modified by increasing or decreasing use. Then, too, other memory circuits could sneak onto the scene by growing nerve fibers that listen in or whisper innuendos. Moreover, human memory can be affected temporarily or even permanently by hormones or other mood-inducing chemicals.

The result of such transformation in the brain is that we seem to recollect only a few types of memories—such as 2 + 2 = 4—exactly the same, time after time. The majority of our memories differ slightly each time we recall them—if only in their associations. This is why our childhood rooms, yards and streets look so much smaller than we once knew them, or why we recite the same incident differently as the years go by, much to the annoyance of our spouses and friends who were there. The memory of a digital computer works quite another way. No matter how many times we use a particular memory location, we receive exactly the same information until the program fills that location with something new.

But precise recollection is not the only difference between human memory and machine memory. Human memory holds things in groups: for example, a name, a face, and various places and experiences we associate with that person. Remembering any part of this group will more than likely bring forth the whole. In a conventional computer, a piece of information can be retrieved only by going through the address of its location, which is either fixed by internal programs or by the programmer's own forethought, and no part of the content of that location can be used to retrieve the whole. Moreover, memories in the brain do not seem confined to discrete locations or cells. They distribute themselves throughout the synapses of various assemblies of neurons. In short, memory in the brain is direct, associative and distributed; in the digital computer it is indirect, disconnected and localized—the difference between eating at a large dinner party with long-time friends or eating alone in a cafeteria.

The Neural Computer

Machines that emulate the brain's neurons and synaptic connections, called neural computers or neural networks, can be built in various ways. For example, neurons and synapses have been simulated mathematically on conventional digital computers, and more recently they have been built with semiconductor materials on chips or by using optical technology with photorefractive crystals.

Like the brain, information in a neural computer is encoded directly in its neural connections rather than in separate memory locations, as is the case with the digital computer; each piece of information is represented by a unique pattern of connections among its artificial neurons. The programmer, or trainer, of a neural computer does not have to give the machine a list of instructions. Instead, the programmer provides enough examples or training data for the machine to set up its unique synaptic patterns. Furthermore, once the machine has been trained, it can receive partial or even somewhat incorrect information and still respond correctly—just as we do.

The ability to learn is another characteristic of neural computers. A child learns to talk by mimicking the words she or he associates with an object or an experience and after a while begins to recognize and make sense of various grammatical patterns. Although no machine exists that can do all of this, some neural computers have made a significant start. To be sure, the kind of learning a neural computer does is primitive, a kind of conditioned response at best. Its ability, however, is not far removed from that of simple animals. This could represent a nascent intelligence capable of learning quite rapidly.

To get an idea of how neural computers work and learn, we turn to a machine dubbed NETtalk, designed by Terry Sejnowski of Johns Hopkins University.[3] NETtalk has only 200 simulated neurons—a fraction of a sea snail's brain power—yet it can teach itself to read aloud. It can just as readily learn to turn speech into text or do something quite different, such as recognize images. If we stood in front of NETtalk at the beginning of its first attempt to articulate a 500-word text transcribed from a first-grader's recorded conversation, we might hear something like this: "Ah-ku-eeeee-mmmuuu-ch-ch-ch-aaaahhhh-eeeeoooo-nunu." After a minute or so the high-pitched, random babble settles into a squall of *m*s and *ah*s: "Mamammaa-mammmmamaaammaamamamamammaamama."

NETtalk has discovered the difference between vowels and consonants. At this stage, it substitutes *m*s for consonants and *ah*s for vowels. If we stay for an hour-and-a-half, we might hear something like: "Kup. Che-ah-mee. Tob ak stub kow wah."

Now it has distinguished individual words and is learning something about sentences. If we leave NETtalk for about ten hours, reading the same text over and over again, constantly correcting itself, this is what we would hear on our return: "I walk home with some friends from school. . . . I like to go to my grandmother's house. Because she gives us . . . candy."[4]

No doubt what we hear is somewhat mechanical and stilted but not

all that different from the way most of us sounded in our first-grade
attempts to read about the adventures of Dick and Jane. Many conventional computers can read texts, but nothing like this. NETtalk has
not been programmed other than to tell it when it has made a mistake,
and after a day of trial-and-error training, it can read its text with 90-
per-cent accuracy. Here is how it happened.

NETtalk was given a table of fifty-three phonetic symbols that represent the various sounds we make from the letter combinations in
the written words. The text is fed into the machine, and the correct
symbols drive a sound system that, in turn, produces speech. The
difference between a neural computer and a conventional computer
lies in how the machines match the letter combinations of the text to
the correct sounds. As we have seen, a conventional computer would
store a program of rules that scans the incoming letter symbols and
selects the correct sounds. There would be a rule, for instance, to
determine whether a vowel was long or short by examining the surrounding vowels and consonants. A conventional computer would
shuffle letters back and forth, fetching and executing its instructions
one after another. It is not learning in even an elementary way. Its
program is telling it what to do.

The neural computer has no such program of instructions. Instead
it has connections between its neuronlike processing elements that
can be strengthened or weakened on a sliding scale according to the
correctness of its responses. With NETtalk all the strengths of the
connections are set at random before the first reading. Letters file in,
and when a particular sound is incorrect, it alters the connections of
the neural elements that produced the error, improving the match. As
it responds to its environment, it programs itself. Any rule the machine discovers, if it can be called that at all, is neither written in
symbolic code nor is it located in a particular place distinct from the
incoming data: it is distributed among all the neuronal connections
simultaneously and automatically.

NETtalk is one of a family of neural computers. To be really effective, neural computers require a tremendous number of neural elements and an even greater number of interconnections. Much processing is required to adjust the strengths of these myriad inter-

connections; problems with the mathematics involved in readjusting the synapses often occur during training sessions. Specialized chips will solve much of this latter difficulty by physically accomplishing what the mathematics does. Still, the ever-present restriction of the vast number of elements and their interconnections remains. Transistors can be placed only so close to each other on a chip before the signals carried along their connecting wires begin to interfere with each other, thereby placing a limit on the density of the processing elements used in semiconductor technology.

Optical Technology

However, one of the most interesting developments in neural-computer architecture—optical technology—promises to relieve this problem. Optical neurons communicate by laser beams, and since light beams can cross each other without interference, optical-processing elements can be packed much more densely than semiconductor transistors. Optical transistors can be made by sandwiching a material such as gallium arsenide between two tiny, partially reflecting mirrors. Such a transistor will not allow light to pass through it unless that light has a certain brightness, or threshold intensity, much as a neuron will not fire unless its interior voltage reaches a certain threshold. Moreover, the reflectivity of its front surface depends on the brightness of the beams hitting its back surface. These properties give optical materials the switching and transmitting capabilities necessary for processing information.

Holograms have the ability to record and then reconstruct the brightness of light, as well as the direction from which it came. This ability makes holograms the most promising devices for establishing and modifying the connections between optical neurons, as well as for storing images, patterns and other information. In principle a three-dimensional crystal hologram with a one-cubic-inch volume can handle more than a trillion connections. The only other system capable of handling information of this magnitude is the brain itself.

Optical technology seems tailor-made for neural computers. Its strengths lie in just those areas that characterize and distinguish neural computers, and its weaknesses lie with those that are less critical for a neural machine, such as logical or computational operations. An experimental optical-pattern-recognition system has already been built at the California Institute of Technology and represents one of the first steps toward building effective optical neural computers. This system, for example, not only recognizes the faces of different people, it can be given a part of an image, say a face from the nose up, and still produce the correct, whole image. Many advances in optical materials, manufacturing technology and understanding brain mechanisms are needed before optical neural computers become practical, let alone challenge the brain. But the potential is there.[5]

Face recognition is important for artificial intelligence. It is an example of a whole class of problems, called random problems (more about these in the next chapter), that have always stymied conventional computers. AI critics have maintained that computers might do some marvelous things, but until they can do what any baby can—find its mother's face from a host of admirers—we can't consider them very intelligent. But the optical neural system is not the only neural computer that waylays this argument.

Consider WIZARD, a non-optical neural network developed by Igor Aleksander and his team at London's Imperial College.[6] When WIZARD is shown pictures of Aleksander's head from only a few angles, it gradually compiles a composite image that enables it to identify him from any perspective. Although a conventional computer can do this in a limited way by storing a digital template of each of the pictures and then comparing any new ones to those in memory, it wouldn't recognize Aleksander unless the expression on his face and the perspective of his head exactly matched one of the stored images. WIZARD, however, because its neuronal connections respond to in-between states, can correctly identify Aleksander from any number of different presentations after studying only a relatively small number of training examples. Moreover, researchers in Finland have devised a neural network that can recognize the photographs of ten people taken from different angles.[7] This system uses the same basic idea of synaptic connections whose strengths can be modified by experience.

In these examples a neural computer can distinguish holistic patterns as complicated and illusive as a human face, even when given a perspective it has never seen before. And, unlike a conventional computer, it doesn't match picture templates in order to find an exact fit.

The Computer Mentality Responds

The computer mentality regards both computers and brains as examples of information-processing machines. It is not particularly concerned with how they operate or their similarities or differences, since it believes intelligence is independent of the particular machine that activates it. Intelligence can be skimmed off the brain's neural substrate and poured into a computer container and processed like so much cream and butter. The computer mentality is not altogether happy with the success of neural computers, however, since they have been able to deal with certain pattern-recognition problems that symbol-manipulating digital computers have not been able to do.

Neural computers are uncomfortably close to biological brains in operation and design, and the computer mentality doesn't want to concede anything to the particular properties of brains since it seeks to divorce intelligence from them. Nevertheless, it maintains that anything the neural computer does can be done, at least in theory, with symbols on the digital computer—only it wouldn't be practical. Indeed, it points out, most neural computers are simulated on conventional computers.

The computer mentality asserts that the digital computer is a universal machine that can symbolize the function and behavior of all machines; furthermore, all intelligence is symbolic in nature even if humans or machines do not understand the symbols. All forms of, and possibilities for, intelligence are encapsuled in symbols, just as everything that happens in the universe can be encapsuled in physical laws or in mathematics, whether we understand them or even know of their existence. Nonetheless, the computer mentality points to the success and potential of both digital and neural computers, and their anticipated union, as irrefutable evidence that intelligence does not arise from the brain alone.

This is a sweeping assertion. The question the computer mentality must address is this: Do biological neurons have special properties that transistors or artificial neurons do not (what philosopher John

Searle calls the brain's causal powers), thereby allowing mental states to arise in the brain that could not possibly arise in a computer? We have in mind such things as sensation, consciousness and intention— matters that have always been closely associated with intelligence. The computer mentality's answer is that there is nothing *unique* about the brain's causal powers, even for these things. It is a slightly stronger version of this statement by Pulitzer Prize winner and computer scientist Douglas Hofstadter:

Minds exist in brains and may come to exist in programmed machines. If and when such machines come about, their causal powers will derive not from the substances they are made of, but from their design and the programs that run in them. And the way we will know they have those causal powers is by talking to them and listening carefully to what they have to say.[8]

The computer mentality, however, has no doubt that minds will come to exist in computers in one form or another. It contends that all mental states originating in the brain can be programmed. We only need to understand exactly what those states are. Consider meaning. Zenon Pylyshyn, a computer scientist at the University of Western Ontario, tries to show how absurd we are to argue otherwise:

If more and more of the cells in your brain were to be replaced by integrated circuit chips, programmed in such a way as to keep the input-output *function* of each unit identical to that of the unit being replaced, you would in all likelihood just keep right on speaking exactly as you are doing now except that you would eventually stop *meaning* anything by it. What we outside observers might take to be words would become for you just certain noises that circuits caused you to make.[9]

Pylyshyn's point is that we would indeed continue to mean what we say even if our brain's become completely transistorized. He is not, of course, seriously suggesting that this could be done; he is asking us to perform a thought experiment. Each individual neuron in the brain, he says, can be simulated on the computer, right down to the chemical reactions, even at the molecular level if necessary. Neurons, chemicals and atoms do certain things to each other that we can measure and represent symbolically, even wetness in the brain. Thus, says the computer mentality, if we replace the neurons in the brain with artificial ones that give exactly the same functional responses as the biological ones, we'd never know the difference, similar to surgeons replacing organs with artificial parts. Under normal circumstances, how many of us can tell if a person has a pacemaker? In a nonstressful situation, even he can't tell the difference. Just because he must take care about doing certain things in no way weakens the argument. It simply means that current pacemakers haven't yet captured all the functions of the heart.

The computer mentality's argument, though it sounds scientific, is not a scientific hypothesis. Any scientific hypothesis worthy of the name must be verifiable. It must be formulated in a way that allows tests to demonstrate its truth or falsity. Short of actually replacing brain neurons with transistors, there is no way of testing the assertion. What if a sophisticated computer with billions of artificial neurons should suddenly announce that it hurts and that it means what it says? How would we know whether to believe it? Hofstadter says that we should talk with it and listen to what it has to say—the Turing Test, in other words. Various philosophers, such as Daniel Dennett, have wondered how they would respond if they found themselves in such a situation. Would they believe it? Yes is the consensus. The computer mentality points out that we aren't in any better position when it comes to knowing if other human beings feel anything or mean what they say. We assume they must because they are like us—intelligent, sentient beings—but there is no way we can really know, other than to believe what we hear. All we have to do, then, to believe that a computer is capable of feeling is to know that it is sufficiently intelligent and complex.

This argument puts the computer mentality in a peculiar position. It says that communication between intelligent beings is an act of faith. The listener must trust in the capability and intention of the speaker, or else certain words mean nothing. At one level the computer mentality asks us to believe that symbols or words have no meaning in themselves, and yet in order to convince us that computers are capable of attaining certain mental states, it turns about and asks us to believe that they mean something. The computer mentality is faced with the obstinate fact that language in some fundamental way depends on a notion as unscientific as credibility.

But how does the computer mentality account for mental states such as sensation, consciousness and intention in biological brains, let alone mechanical ones? Why is it that individual neurons, like transistors, can feel nothing at all, yet humans feel while computers don't?

The explanation? It depends on the nature of collective phenomena—things that can only happen in large groups of individuals and can't happen in smaller ones. Physicist John Hopfield explains such phenomena in this way: put two molecules in a box and watch them collide, which doesn't often happen. Now put in a thousand more; we have more collisions than before, but the interactions are basically the same as when we had two. Now put in a billion billion molecules and we have something new—sound waves—coming from a degree of organization that would not have been possible with fewer molecules. Nothing in the collision of two molecules would remotely suggest anything like sound waves, which can't exist without enough collisions to keep the waves organized. Many of the phenomena arising in thermodynamics, hydrodynamics and magnetism are likewise collective in nature.[10]

The computer mentality holds that just as sound emerges from the interactions of billions of soundless individual molecules, so sensation, consciousness and intention arise from the interactions of billions of insensate processing units, whether in brains or computers—provided there are enough of them organized in the right way. Computers don't yet have nearly enough, nor do we know how to organize them. We don't even know enough about collective phenomena to determine at what point of complexity new qualities emerge. But sensation, consciousness and intention are no more mysterious than vast collections of particles acting in concert to produce sound waves.

The Larger Agenda
The computer mentality would face a major obstacle if it attempted to create an artificial mind by modeling the brain in silicon, lasers or any other material. The brain is simply too complex and too little

understood for anyone to explain how it gives rise to intelligence. So the computer mentality attempts to avoid the problem altogether by postulating that intelligence is not a matter of the brain at all. It asserts that we need not wait centuries until we understand all of the brain's biological and chemical intricacies; we must simply construct some kind of machine that rivals the brain in producing intelligent behavior.

But why is the computer mentality so adamant about being able to separate all the activities and qualities of intelligence from the brain and from the total human being? There is a certain unmistakable militancy surrounding the computer mentality's agenda of emulating the brain's abilities on machines, an urgency that contains within it more than the spirit of disinterested scientific inquiry or the passion to know and understand ourselves.

The answer, in good measure, is that the computer mentality wants to do its part in being true to the scientific faith by which it lives and breathes. Scientism depends on a materialistic view of the cosmos where all things can be measured and manipulated; thus hope lies in scientific breakthroughs and technological advances. This enterprise has the added dimension of needing to dispel the notion of God in the minds of all informed and reasonable people. Perhaps by showing that creatures can re-create the most complicated part of creation, they can thereby show that they have no need for God in their attempts at solving the mysteries of the cosmos.

Even so, the computer mentality knows it must be satisfied with an analogy for the human brain since it cannot hope to create an actual one. And it has to push its analogy hard, for as neurophysiologist William Calvin observes: "Without analogies, it is indeed hard to imagine us humans happening without design—and so one is led to suspect some sort of cosmic principle, if not the guiding hand of a Creator, shaping evolution towards complexity. And us."[11] This the computer mentality will not grant.

For many Christians the goal of the computer mentality in designing a machine to rival the brain is megalomania. But we must remember that the computer mentality need not actually accomplish all its vision to make its point. It will be enough to convince this and the next few generations that we differ in no essential way from manmade computers, that we are mere biological computers with no divine maker. There is not much doubt that a combination of digital and neural computers will give rise to machines that do indeed act with intelligence and that can learn from experience. Exactly what kind of intelligence is hard to say, but perhaps we can catch a glimpse of it by looking at what has been accomplished already.

4
CREATING
INTELLIGENCE

No one really knows how human intelligence works; so we can hardly expect to fare any better when we turn to artificial intelligence. For example, getting machines to do complex math computations or play a good game of chess was once considered intelligent behavior on the part of computers; indeed, they were often called super brains. Today no one considers such tasks to involve real intelligence—at least not the way most computers accomplish them. We now believe that such things as recognizing faces and understanding language, difficult tasks for a conventional computer, require more true intelligence. Yet, even none-too-bright people can do these things well; even animals can do some of them.

We are almost forced into having one set of criteria for machines, one for animals and one for humans. This does not set well with the computer mentality, which believes that intelligence is symbolic in nature and universal in scope. The problem, it counters, is that when we understand what lies behind an intelligent activity—that is, as soon as we can write down precise rules that generate it—then we no longer think it requires intelligence, especially in machines—and this is unfair.

Nevertheless, nearly everyone agrees that intelligence involves logic, pattern recognition and the ability to change actions, behavior and thoughts in response to changes in the physical, intellectual or social environment. An intelligent being should grow in its repertoire of responses, make new associations and set new goals for itself. In this chapter we will give a brief overview of what has been accomplished thus far in machine intelligence, some of the problems it has encountered, and some examples of its failures and successes.

To begin, we need to qualify what was said about neural computers being a recent development in artificial intelligence; they are new only in their present form. Since the 1940s researchers dreamed of building machines designed after the brain—machines with on/off neurons, firing thresholds and weighted connections between them. In 1957 Frank Rosenblatt, a Cornell Aeronautical Laboratory scientist, used electrical components to build one of the first neural computers, calling it the "perceptron." Because of the difficulties of wiring its neural circuits and modifying the strengths of the connections between its neurons, researchers simulated later models of the perceptron with programs on conventional digital computers. By the 1960s, hundreds of people were designing perceptronlike machines—and not getting far.

In 1969 Marvin Minsky and Seymour Papert of MIT published *Perceptrons,* a book in which they demonstrated mathematically that perceptrons could only deal with a limited number of simple tasks. Moreover, they proved that if you tried to overcome their limitations with more complicated neuronal connections, they wouldn't learn anything.

The Arrival of Expert Systems
Interest in perceptrons died almost instantly, replaced by AI programs known as expert systems. These programs run on conventional com-

puters and are radically different from the brain-modeling approach of neural computers. Expert systems are programs that are supposed to perform expertly in limited areas, as human experts do. The dream is to program these systems to perform as well as, if not better than, their human counterparts. How? First, programmers pack them full of textbook knowledge. Next, a "knowledge engineer" interviews human experts in the field, getting them to explain all the intuitive rules of thumb and exceptions they use in making decisions.

A good example is a medical program that diagnoses diseases. Stored in its memory is a tremendous amount of information, perhaps far more than any human head could hold, as well as a number of complicated inferencing rules. Provided with a list of symptoms along with the results of a patient's medical history and tests, the program will suggest possible causes and even assign probabilities to each. Some expert systems are capable of carrying on a limited, free-form conversation with their users.

Medicine is just one area where expert systems are used. Most commercial applications of artificial intelligence are found in financial planning, education, computer design, chemistry, surveying, and oil exploration and drilling.[1]

Although researchers have worked with expert systems for more than two decades, they have not made the progress they anticipated. There is good reason for that, say philosopher Hubert Dreyfus and his mathematician brother Stuart, long-time critics of artificial intelligence, particularly expert systems. Although they have won some battles and lost others, they delivered a telling blow to expert systems in their book *Mind over Machine: The Power of Human Intuition and Expertise in the Era of the Computer.*

The problem with expert systems, they say, is inadvertently exposed by Edward Feigenbaum, the developer of DENDRAL (one of the most interesting and successful expert systems around, which uses mass spectrography to analyze the molecular structures of a limited class of chemical compounds). Feigenbaum says that the knowledge engineer is supposed to sit down with the experts and "mine those jewels of knowledge out of their heads one by one."[2] But as soon as the knowledge engineer thinks he finds a bona fide rule of thumb or nugget of genuine wisdom, the expert says, " 'That's true, but if you see enough patients/rocks/chip designs/instrument readings, you see that it isn't true after all.' . . . At this point, knowledge threatens to become ten thousand special cases."[3]

This is why expert systems are doomed from the start, say the Dreyfuses. We do not become experts by starting with lots of specific cases and then developing abstract rules to encompass the particulars. The reverse is true: beginners start with abstract rules and become experts by discerning through experience and pattern recognition all kinds of special cases. By asking an expert to explain herself by rules, the knowledge engineer is asking her to revert to a beginner's way of looking at things, which she can't do without violating everything that makes her an expert.

According to the Dreyfuses, a person goes through five stages in becoming an expert: novice, advanced beginner, competent, proficient and expert. What stands out in the various stages is the "progression *from* the analytic behavior of a detached subject, consciously decomposing his environment into recognizable elements, and following abstract rules, *to* involved skilled behavior based on an accumulation of concrete experiences and the unconscious recognition of new situations as similar to whole remembered ones."[4] There is nothing mystical about this—it's the way the brain works. Any situation triggers circuits of neurons whose synaptic connections are reinforced through repetition and experience. The situation has directly affected the machinery of the brain, and there are no rules or symbols involved.

According to the Dreyfuses, expert systems bring machine intelligence to somewhere between the advanced beginner and the competent level. The higher levels will remain out of reach for conventional symbol-manipulating machines, since a proficient performer leaves symbols and rules behind and relies on intuition.

Does this mean that expert systems have no place? Not at all—so long as the applications don't require more than a smattering of natural language, understanding, common sense and the ability to adjust to unanticipated changes. Expert systems show promise *only* in those areas involving so much information that not even humans can reach the expert level of holistic pattern recognition, or those certain kinds of time-consuming, routine tasks that nevertheless require extensive, precise, logical analysis.

Back to Neural Computers

Except in one important area that we will examine shortly, AI research seemed to stall a little less than a decade ago—until 1982 when John Hopfield, a biophysicist at Caltech and Bell Laboratories, showed how to design neural computers that overcome the limitations pointed out by Minsky and Papert. He and other researchers created more sophisticated neurons than were used in the old perceptrons. The output of the new neurons can respond on a sliding scale to changes in their input, unlike the perceptron's neurons, which had to be either on or off. The strengths of the neuronal connections can be adjusted more easily, accurately and systematically than before. Moreover, the perceptron's input neurons were connected directly to its output neurons, making it behave in a knee-jerk, reflex-action fashion, whereas the new neural computers have a layer of hidden, in-between neurons that make their responses much more flexible. Minsky admits that his earlier criticism of the whole neural approach was a case of overkill. But, he cautions, the new machines do not escape all the limitations of the old perceptrons; for example, they tend to settle on solutions that aren't always the best ones. Nevertheless, he predicts that neural computers will come into their own in about a decade. Even the ever-skeptical Dreyfus brothers are impressed. After making a cautionary, it's-too-early-to-tell disclaimer, they say: "A computational device with these abilities [such as pattern recognition and learning] would represent a monumental step toward a genuine artificial intelligence."[5]

Neural computers don't exist only on drawing boards or in experimental laboratories. Several companies are already realizing their commercial value.[6] Yet some AI experts think the technology is not nearly ready to commercialize. Others warn that computer companies that don't offer neural networks won't be around in five years. Venture capitalists, computer manufacturers, the military and even insurance companies are investing in companies that either build neural computers with specialized chips or use programs and boards that plug into conventional personal computers. The applications range from speech recognition and artificial vision to factory automation and product control to recognizing handwriting on insurance forms and checks. Some of these products are already on the market and sell in the range of $1,000 to $15,000. In the near future neural computers will be used for security systems and satellite surveillance, as well as a host of military applications, such as spotting camouflaged tanks or supporting sophisticated Star Wars systems.

But neural computers aren't the only hope for artificial intelligence. As we mentioned, there is an area where progress is being made with programs on the conventional digital computer; namely, the development of language-understanding programs. One of the key people behind this research is Roger Schank, head of Yale University's AI laboratory.

Understanding Language

Schank is one of AI's most respected figures. An entire school of research has sprung from the products of his imagination, and his students hold prominent positions in some of the country's most prestigious laboratories. For Schank, artificial intelligence is just a new term for the study of the mind, and the way to the mind is through language. Schank didn't enter the field because he was fascinated with computers. He became one of the world's foremost AI researchers because he was fascinated with people: he is a psychologist, first and last. Understandably, he gets annoyed when the media give the impression that expert systems are what AI is all about. His condemnation is swift and sure: "Like most AI terms, the words 'expert system' are loaded with a great deal more implied intelligence than is warranted by their actual level of sophistication."[7]

Somewhat like the Dreyfus scale for expertness, Schank has a scale for understanding language which goes from MAKING SENSE to COGNITIVE UNDERSTANDING and, finally, COMPLETE EMPATHY. At the MAKING SENSE level, we fit things together into some kind of coherent structure, though in a restricted way. Consider, for example, the sentence "Bill cried when Mary said she loved John."

If we were operating at the MAKING SENSE level, we would understand that Bill was sad and then try to determine some of the circumstances that connect Bill, Mary and John. Bill is sad because he probably loves Mary, and she doesn't love him. But does John love Mary? At the COMPLETE EMPATHY level, however, we would say, "I know exactly how Bill must have felt. That happened to me with Sue and Pete. It took me a year to get over it."

Computers will never reach COMPLETE EMPATHY, says Schank, but some can already interpret stories at the MAKING SENSE level. They will eventually attain COGNITIVE UNDERSTANDING. Then they will be able to learn or change by comparing their present experiences to those in the past and noticing important relationships. Furthermore, computers will generate new information from these experiences and be able to explain how they arrived at their conclusions. Schank is not talking about neural computers here; he is thinking of programs running on conventional computers. He estimates that if it doesn't happen within our lifetime, it will during our children's. Then, too, the situation could change fast if Schank's programs were combined with the brainlike abilities of neural computers. One way or the other, we need to know what Schank and his coworkers are doing, how they search for machine intelligence and how close they have come to finding it.

The history of language-understanding programs has been an up-and-down affair. Thirty years ago there was a great deal of interest in machine translation of texts from one language to another. But language is tricky. There is the problem of sentences that mean the same thing but have different structures: "John likes music" and "Music pleases John" or "John is pleased by music." Then there are sentences with the same structure but radically different meanings: "John touched the dog with the long stick" and "John touched the dog with the long hair." Or one sentence that could mean a couple of things: "Flying planes can be dangerous" or "He was too old to help." The ambiguity of language is a horror to the literal-minded computer: "He gave me an apple," "He gave his best," "He gave me the creeps," "He gave up." And so machine translation was given up as a lost cause.

Nevertheless, language is the key to understanding, thought

Schank. To get around its vagaries, he started at the bottom, developing eleven primitive notions that can be combined in different ways to represent all actions and all meanings. Here are some examples.

ATRANS is the transfer of anything abstract, such as the possession or control involved in giving, taking or buying. PTRANS is the physical transfer of an object, as in walking, going, riding or putting. MTRANS means the transfer of mental concepts or information, as in talking or writing. MBUILD is the processing of information or thinking. Then there is ATTEND: paying attention with the eyes or ears. PROPEL is the application of a force, such as pushing or kicking.

In a way Schank seems presumptuous—condensing everything from Shakespeare to the Bible to combinations of eleven concepts. But he is interested in plain, not fancy. He wants the computer to be able to understand and use human language, and yet he knows it will fall short. Nevertheless, he hopes to give his programs a bit of genuine understanding; once having done that much, he knows he can increase understanding. Not that the computer will ever possess human understanding, but that it will have some kind of intelligence, and then some kind of super intelligence. Here is a simple example of how his scheme works, using the sentence "John sold Mary a book." Its internal representation looks something like this:

ACTION:	ATRANS		
ACTOR:	John		
OBJECT:	book	ACTION:	ATRANS
TO:	Mary ———————	ACTOR:	Mary
FROM:	John	OBJECT:	money
		TO:	John
		FROM:	Mary

Our sentence involves two transfers, a book and money, one in each direction between two people. This is why the two ATRANSs are linked together. ATRANS sets up expectations of an actor, an object and the movements to and from. These blanks must be filled in by the context of the sentence, whether they are mentioned explicitly or not. This internal structure enables a computer to make inferences based on these expectations as well as the context in which the sentence occurs. For example, we know that Mary now possesses the book and John the money. Perhaps John didn't need the book because he had already read it. Or maybe he had to have money for some reason. Mary doesn't have as much money as she did before. These are some of the inferences and conjectures that ATRANS sets up.

The sentence "Burt gave Joe a black eye for calling him a name" would not use ATRANS but a combination of MTRANS and PROPEL. Joe MTRANSed a mental concept, a name, to Burt who PROPELs his fist into Joe's eye. The computer knows that when a PROPEL is linked to an animate object, it should expect a change of its HEALTH, one of the states or conditions of animate objects, or it might link name-calling to ANGER, another state of animate objects. The computer functions at the MAKING SENSE level by being able to answer questions like "Why did Burt get angry?" or "How far apart were Joe and Burt when this happened?" It also expects that Joe might hit back.

Much of common sense has to do with plausible inferences, which we seldom consider because they are too obvious to mention. In one of his earliest programs, Schank used Chuck Rieger's work on inferencing. As part of his doctoral dissertation at Stanford University, Rieger found sixteen general classes of inferences that can be drawn from the meanings of various sentences. We can derive these inferences from basic assumptions about the real world.[8] Here are some examples of sentences and inferences:

A Specification Inference: John picked up the bat. He hit the ball. Inference: He hit the ball with the bat.

A Causative Inference: John slammed the book down on the table. Inference: John was probably upset.

A Resultative Inference: John gave Bill an apple. Inference: Bill has the apple.

An Enablement Inference: John bought an apple. Inference: John had to have money.

A Function Inference: John got his hammer and nails. Inference:

He wants to build or fix something.

A Feature Inference: John wears size-three shoes. Inference: John is a child.

Using these sixteen rules as well as his primitive notions of ATRANS, MTRANS and so forth, Schank and his coworkers developed MARGIE, the first program that could paraphrase meanings and translate and draw inferences from individual, unrelated sentences. Although he needed surprisingly little grammar to translate these sentences into his system of primitive concepts, Schank had two immediate problems to deal with in MARGIE: it drew so many inferences that they clogged up the works, and the inferences were so far removed from the point that they were ridiculous. In addition, MARGIE was unable to relate one sentence to another in a larger context.

For a year Schank considered these problems. His partial solution handled both problems simultaneously. Most of the contexts we encounter are stereotypical situations to which we respond in more or less standard ways. Why not think of ourselves as actors in a play following scripts and using props? This, thought Schank, would reduce the number and irrelevancy of the inferences the machine would make, as well as provide it with a well-connected background in which it could link sentences. So Schank, along with Yale psychologist Robert Abelson, invented the notion of scripts. SAM (Script Applier Mechanism) was born.

From MARGIE to SAM

A standard example of a script is a restaurant sketch. The main characters are the customer, the waitress and the cook; the props are tables, the menu, the check and money. When the curtain rises we find a hungry customer with money. At the finale, the customer is no longer hungry and has less money, while the restaurateur has more. In scene one, the customer enters the restaurant, looks at the tables, picks one, goes to it and sits down. Scene two covers the details of ordering, which include the entrance of the waitress and her order to the cook. In scene three the waitress brings the food and the customer eats it. Being a four-scene, one-act play, it saves the best for the last: the dramatic exit of our hero after he receives the check, leaves the tip and pays the cashier.

This is just a brief synopsis, of course, of all the interactions with the knife, fork, plate, the bill, the money and the customer and the waitress. We don't have to be astute drama critics to see that this play is just one of an entire genre of restaurant scripts. Other scripts might have a customer wait to be seated at a fancy restaurant or have him go directly to the counter in a fast-food restaurant. We can have scripts within scripts, that is, programs within programs.

Schank designed scripts to enable computers to understand stories. Suppose we gave this scenario to a computer equipped with an appropriate restaurant script: "John went to a restaurant and ordered a hamburger. He paid the check and left." Nowhere do we say that John ate the hamburger. But common sense tells us that he did; likewise, the script must tell the computer. Did he leave a tip and pick up the check? Without information to the contrary, the computer would answer that he probably did. The script fills in the holes. This is an example of what computer programmers call a default assumption: unless something happens to the contrary, the program, by default, follows a certain predetermined course.

But suppose something peculiar happens: "John goes to a restaurant and orders a hamburger. By the time the waitress brings his order, the burger is stone cold, and he leaves her a very small tip." All four scenes in our original play are represented, but there are two deviations from the normal script—the cold burger and the small tip. The computer infers that the customer is not satisfied. Working backward from the ATRANS concept of an unusually small transfer of money, it is able to link the small tip to the cold hamburger via the actor's displeasure. If we asked the computer why John left a small tip, it would be able to reply that his hamburger was cold.

Scripts work well for stereotypical situations and go a long way toward supplying a computer with a semblance of common sense. But an intelligent computer must deal with situations for which there are no scripts. So how do we humans handle circumstances we have never before encountered? We certainly don't ignore all the scripts we carry with us, but like jazz musicians or actors we must improvise by putting our formulaic materials together in new and interesting ways. But what is it that enables us to link pieces of information together for which no rules or prescribed patterns exist? Schank says we have goals that determine how we act and shape events. When actors improvise, they must have something to go on, goals to help direct their actions. Once actors have their goals in mind, they must then plan how to put them in action.

Because people have many types of goals, Schank needed a scheme for them, just as he needed a system to represent thoughts. So he classified goals under a few general categories; for example, the goal to change the state of something he called CHANGE-GOALS. Under this category, Schank included changing proximity or position, changing control, changing knowledge, power or authority, as well as getting someone else to pursue a goal in our stead. He then determined various plans we use to achieve our goals: for instance, if we are to change our position, we may use a private vehicle, use public transportation, use animals or use ourselves. For goals involving control, authority or influence over others, we often use persuasion. We might simply ask for what we want, appeal to reason or bargain with an object or favor. Some people might even threaten or overpower another person to get what they want.

Let's see how this works by considering another scenario: "John glanced anxiously at his watch. He didn't have much time to get to the theater and put on his make-up for his very first professional performance. He hurriedly dug in his pockets. Blast! No money for cab fare. He turned to Mary."

John wants to get to the theater, a CHANGE-PROXIMITY goal. His plan is to use PUBLIC TRANSPORTATION (a cab). A subgoal is to CHANGE-CONTROL of money, so he turns to Mary with the idea of using some kind of PERSUASION plan to accomplish it. He might use any of the following:

ASK: Would you please give me the cab fare?

INVOKE THEME: After all I've gone through for years to get here, it would be a shame to miss my big opportunity because of cab fare—besides, you are my sister.

INFORM REASON: I may never have another chance at a role like this one.

BARGAIN OBJECT: I'll exchange this front-row ticket for the fare.

BARGAIN FAVOR: I'll fix your leaky faucets.

THREATEN: If you don't, it's curtains for us.

This is just a glance at some of the ways goals and plans fit together. Schank knows that life is not so simple. Any system that purports to be intelligent would have to know that humans have needs for food, shelter, clothing, sleep and love. It must know about priorities—for example, the difference between our longing for food when we are stranded in a blizzard and when we are prowling the kitchen for a late-night snack. This means that we often have conflicting goals that constantly demand resolution.

TALE-SPIN
While Schank and his coworkers were investigating how people plan and achieve their goals, they created TALE-SPIN, a fascinating program that was the first to make up its own stories. It knew a few principles of good story-telling, made up characters, put them in situations and created conflicts for them. None of the stories is canned; no sentences or fragments of the story were programmed in advance.

James Meehan, the principal creator of TALE-SPIN and one of Schank's students, wanted it to create Aesop-type fables. One of the problems he faced was to get a character to notice the actions of other characters without having them actually talk to each other. Here is a sample of one of TALE-SPIN's early attempts to produce something like Aesop's "The Ant and the Dove":

Henry Ant was thirsty. He walked over to the river bank where his good friend Bill Bird was sitting. Henry slipped and fell in the river.

He was unable to call for help. He drowned.

This little tragedy was not supposed to happen. Falling in the river was introduced as the central conflict; yet Bill was supposed to save Henry. But Henry's MTRANS (transfer of mental concepts or information) for speech had been written so that water would prevent his yelling. Since Henry couldn't address Bill directly, Bill had no way of noticing the problem.

So Meehan programmed his characters to notice something that undergoes an unusual change of position. Here are a few rules in the program: if A moves B to location C, then both A and B are at C; if somebody falls, it is because gravity moved that character; if someone is in the river, eventually he will have to get out by swimming or flying or asking for help—else he will drown. Meehan tried his program again.

Henry Squirrel was thirsty. He walked over to the river bank where his good friend Bill Bird was sitting. Henry slipped and fell in the river. Gravity drowned.

This was absolutely logical. The programmed translated "Henry fell" as "gravity moved Henry." When gravity moved Henry into the water, they are both there together—remember the first rule above—and both of them must get out or drown. But poor gravity doesn't have legs or wings or friends to help it out. So while Bill sits obliviously on the bank, gravity drowns, and we don't know what happens to Henry. Meehan corrected this problem by interpreting "fall" as the result of a force *acting on* an object rather than one moving with the object.[9]

The work at Yale goes on, each new advance turning up a host of new problems. Scripts, goals and plans all constitute a large part of intelligence, says Schank, but these alone do not enable the computer to reach COGNITIVE UNDERSTANDING. He thinks that the more sophisticated programs do MAKE SENSE of stories, but he considers none of them very intelligent, because his idea of intelligence is the ability to react to something new in a nonprogrammed way. Intelligent machines must have common sense, dynamic memories and the ability to profit from experience. In other words, computers must be able to learn; they must bring the past to bear on the present. New experience must not only add to or subtract from a computer's memory; it must also change the connections or associations in that memory—just as it happens in our brains.

Until a computer is affected by what happens to it, which will occur in large part when one thing reminds it of something else, it cannot be called intelligent. Schank uses the example of *West Side Story* and *Romeo and Juliet* to make his point. Although the Renaissance setting of Shakespeare's tragedy about two rival families bears little immediate resemblance to a musical about a New York gang war, an intelligent computer should recognize the theme that underlies both: two people are denied happiness because they belong to hostile groups.

Similarity is not the only way we are reminded of other things. Sometimes an event triggers remembrances because it fails to measure up to our expectations. Suppose we try an unfamiliar restaurant and find exceptionally good food at a moderate price. Normally we expect to pay high prices for exceptional food and middling prices for middling food. Because our experience with this restaurant falls outside our usual expectations, we are reminded of other restaurants and other meals where the same thing happened. Someone, either we or the management, has made a sort of error—and, according to Schank, these kinds of errors, along with those that are genuine mistakes, are central to how we learn. Errors force us to shift our attention and focus on what is important. They change the way our memories are organized, creating nodes at the places where the failures occurred, so that from then on we will take a different route through the web of our remembrances.

Some of the programs developed at Yale do reorganize themselves because of failure or changes in anticipated circumstances. They are crude learners that can develop primitive, unsophisticated beliefs. Only recently, says Schank, have researchers begun writing programs that have reminding ability. Although they do not come close to modeling human intelligence, progress is being made—and without providing them too much knowledge at the outset.

Random Problems
The question still remains: How much information does a computer need to behave intelligently? Although this question is too big to deal

with in its entirety, there is an important class of problems whose solutions apparently elude conventional digital-computer programs. Researchers use the word *random* to describe these kinds of problems. A random problem is characterized by its open-endnesses; that is, there is no way to list all the information necessary for its solution, nor are there any precise formulas that guarantee an answer in a finite number of steps—both of which the conventional computer must have in order to come to a solution. A classic example of a random problem is recognizing a tree. Obviously humans can solve this problem, but not by knowing all the angles of the branches and leaf stems or all of the tree shapes and colors, or even by applying mathematical formulas—all things the conventional computer needs to do its work. We recognize a tree without having in mind a precise description of every tree in the world and then matching the one in front of us with all those we remember until we hit an exact match.

So the answer to the question as to how much information a conventional computer needs to do such an apparently simple thing as recognize a tree seems to be this: too much. Other examples of random problems are recognizing faces, fingerprints and handwriting— the solutions to which also require the ability to recognize patterns. This means, in part, the ability to pick out a particular individual from an undifferentiated background, or to recognize different appearances of the same individual—for example, a person with different hair styles—or further, to put similar individuals in a group—all of which, as we mentioned, neural computers can already do.

So what is it that gives neural computers the ability to deal with this kind of problem, whereas conventional computers cannot? Part of the answer lies in the difference between how the memories of the two machines work. John Hopfield, who was largely responsible for the recent revival of neural computers, explains it this way: neural computers have contours like a mountainous countryside complete with valleys and lakes. If we pour a bucket of water anywhere on elevated ground in the countryside, it will eventually flow into a low-lying lake.

The lake, says Hopfield, represents a stable state of precise information. If a drop of water falls on a mountainside near a lake in a valley, it will follow a flow line down to that lake. The unstable droplet is like a piece of incomplete information leading to the full, stable information of the lake, which, in turn, is like a state of memory in a neural net. So if we start anywhere near one of these flow lines of memory, we will eventually find the complete memory. The topography of the countryside—its contours and elevations—is defined by the strengths of the connections between the artificial neurons in the network. These variable connections are what give the underlying shape to the flow of information that eventually settles into a stable memory enabling a neural network to deal with fragmentary, imprecise data and to recognize the similarities between patterns.[10]

Extending Hopfield's analogy, we can see how information could separate into several flow lines and come to rest in many different lake-memories—similar to the way a piece of information fans out in our brains, triggering a host of associated memories. This is not what happens in a digital computer, which must be given a precise address in order to locate an isolated piece of information—one of the reasons why it is so difficult to give a conventional machine an associative memory or to program it to deal with random problems. But this same restriction is also what gives the digital computer its ability to manipulate individual symbols quickly and accurately and to perform intricate logical computations—things that pose difficulties for the pattern-recognizing neural computer.

One of the developments in the field of artificial intelligence is the effort to bring the two types of machines together, thus overcoming their weaknesses. Researchers are trying to give conventional computers reminding ability or associative memories, whereas others are trying to make their neural machines more precise and logical. Yet how close are we to machines that seem to have some of the cognitive and psychological characteristics of people?

The Work of James Anderson

To get at least a partial answer to this question, we can turn to the work of cognitive scientist James Anderson of Brown University. Anderson explores how far neural computers approximate humans in how we seem to do logic (as contrasted to the way digital computers do it), the way we are able to select a prototypical individual from a group of similar individuals (the way we categorize or stereotype), how we are able to deal with partial or contradictory information (our ability to live in an imperfect world) and how our brains still function while suffering neuronal loss (our brain's robustness).[11]

Using a conventional computer, Anderson simulated a fifty-neuron network that learns words and concepts and puts them together in patterns resembling logical syllogisms. He has taught a machine to behave logically, in a limited way, by example and association, instead of programming it with the formal rules of logic.

His aim was to get his neural net to do syllogisms, as illustrated by the most famous of them all: Socrates is a man; men are mortal; therefore Socrates is mortal. He began by teaching his system ten words, each of which he gave a unique pattern. The words he taught the machine were *Socrates, Alcibiades* (Athenian general, politician and friend of Socrates), *Plato, Zeus, Apollo, Diane, man, god, mortal, immortal.* He used sixteen neurons for the proper names, another sixteen for man/god, and another sixteen for mortal/immortal.

Initially, Anderson set the strengths of the synapses between the neurons at random, and then presented the words to the system at random for 500 learning trials. He modified the strengths of the synapses by a mathematical technique that considers the difference between what the output ought to be and what it actually is—a process repeated until the output pattern matches the input pattern and the memory of the word is distributed throughout the synapses.

Because many different words used the same neurons, the training process was somewhat tricky. For example, suppose we taught the system the word *Socrates,* and then we turn to teaching it *Plato.* In readjusting the synapses for *Plato,* we disturb the proper settings for *Socrates.* Anderson circumvented this problem by the way he initially coded the words. A special mathematical structure called *orthogonal coding,* which is built into the way the words are patterned in the machine, helped clear up the memory interference. (All simulated neural networks have this problem, and it is resolved more or less satisfactorily in various ways. This difficulty will probably be alleviated with the development of special neuronal-type chips, or by holograms in the case of optical neural computers.)

After having taught the machine individual words, Anderson, in 1,000 random trials, taught the machine to associate pairs of words by superimposing their individual patterns on each other, such as *Socrates-man, Plato-man, Zeus-god, Apollo-god, man-mortal, god-immortal*. The entire training process took about five minutes (if the system were built of specialized chips instead of being simulated, it would take a matter of seconds). At this point Anderson had taught the machine the premises of syllogisms: *Socrates-man, man-mortal* or *Zeus-god, god-immortal*. But he had not trained it to make the association *Socrates-man-mortal*, the logical conclusion of the premises. Nevertheless, the machine supplied this missing information itself by means of its superimposed patterns.

Anderson's system used a mixture of pluses, minuses and dots to produce its patterns, which we on the outside of the machine translate into pidgin English, such as *Socrates-man*. But suppose we hooked it up with a Schanklike language program that could generate grammatically correct sentences from the patterns? Although Anderson hasn't yet done this, it wouldn't be difficult; such hybrids could make simple but accurate English translations of what Anderson's machine produced in pattern form.

We say to the system, "Socrates is a man, and Zeus is a god. What can you tell me?"

The machine replies, "Socrates is mortal, and Zeus is immortal."

"Do you know Herb?"

"No. Who or what is Herb?"

"Herb is a man. What can you tell me about Herb?"

"I'm still not sure about Herb, but whoever he is, he is mortal."

Anderson reports that when he gave his system the name "Herb," which it had not previously learned, it made the correct inference even though the pattern for Herb was only partial because it contained some unresolved elements. This is similar to our ability to un erstand pi cemeal i for ation. The machine is also able to do this because an overall pattern is precipitated by a fragment of itself, even a fragment that is not quite accurate—reminiscent of Hopfield's analogy of a drop of water falling close to a flow-line and running down into a lake.

Clearly, says Anderson, this system is not doing formal logic: no set of predetermined rules guarantees a correct answer every time. However, it is not clear that humans do formal logic, either. Most people need extensive training in the mechanics of correct symbol manipulation, and we use aids such as diagrams and machines to help us. Human reason relies on memory association and analogy. As such, says Anderson, neural models are much more similar to humans in cognitive ability than they are to conventional digital computers.

There is yet another human ability that neural computers seem to have that digital computers don't. Linguists and psychologists are finding evidence that when we form categories of objects or concepts, some objects are more representative of a particular class than others. Think of a bird. Chances are good that you pictured something that looks more like a robin or sparrow than a stork or buzzard. Another example is the way humans think of color. Anthropologists have shown samples of various shades of red to people all over the world. When these people are asked to choose the "best" example of red, all the subjects picked the same sample, regardless of their language or culture. It seems that members of a category tend to cluster around these dynamic prototypes—these special individuals that seem to organize the whole. The explanation may have something to do with the way prototypical individuals set off stronger neuronal patterns and more rapid firing frequencies in the brain than those triggered by others in the same category.

This runs counter to the traditional logical-mathematical view, which defines categories as collections of objects whose common properties make all individuals equal so that none of them stands out. This definition fits nicely in the conventional computer's world of rules and symbols. A conventional computer cannot automatically designate one individual out of a group as being more representative unless it has been programmed to do so.

But Anderson reports a different situation with the neural computer. He devised an experiment that showed how humans pick out certain prototypical patterns from groups of related ones. Nine randomly distributed dots were used as prototypical patterns to generate nine different families of related offspring by shifting the dots a slight distance from their original positions in the parent pattern. When people were shown a hodgepodge of patterns from the different families, they learned to sort them into their correct categories without actually seeing the parent prototypes that generated all the patterns. After learning to recognize the families, they were given a test of random examples and asked to classify them. Some of the test patterns they had seen before, some were newly generated from the original prototypes, and some were the original prototypes themselves. People classified the prototypes more quickly and accurately than they did the derived patterns, even believing that they had seen the prototypes before when, in fact, they hadn't. Anderson ran the same experiment using a neural computer in place of the human subjects. When the test data of both human and machine performance were compared, the results were strikingly similar, the computer running roughly 15 per cent behind the human subjects in accuracy in picking out the prototypes.

The same sort of thing showed up in Anderson's name/species/life span neural network—the one he used for his logic experiment described above. The machine was taught to associate various names with the concepts man and god, but it had not been taught to make the reverse association. The machine had not been taught to single out prototypical individuals in each general category. Here is what happened—again, we are translating an imaginary conversation using a Schanklike translator, but the results are quite accurate:

"What name do you associate with a god?"

"Zeus."

"Give me the name you associate with mortal man."

"+-+-+-+++---+-++" (the pattern the machine actually produced).

"Give me a name for this pattern."

"OK. Joe is its name."

"So Joe is the name you associate with mortal man?"

"Yes."

Zeus, a name that the machine had previously learned, has become the prototypical god, says Anderson, whereas the prototypical man was not any of the names it had learned. Anderson's machine formed its own stereotypes just as you or I might; it may turn out that each neural computer has its own peculiar idiosyncrasies. Whether by fluke or not, these machines seem able to form unexpected predilections from associations they have learned on the basis of their experience. This is disconcertingly close to the way we humans operate.

In the previous chapter we explained that a neural computer can recognize different presentations of a person's face even though it has never seen them before. It has the ability, that is, to see many things as being equivalent without having been told they are. This means the neural computer can form a general category from a group of similar individuals and correctly identify new instances of the category when it sees them. Once having formed a category, it can select an individual that best represents the category. To be sure, the experimental results are isolated and fragmentary; no single machine has been constructed that incorporates all these abilities. Yet there is something new here, something that may represent the beginnings of a true artificial intelligence, the arrival of a machine that can abstract and generalize from its own experience.

Before we leave Anderson's neural computer, we need to consider another of its brainlike features—its robustness. Anderson studied the effect of damage on his fifty-neuron machine's ability to recognize various line segments when presented at different angles. He proceeded to destroy in 4-per-cent chunks the network's synaptic connections. The results? No change in the machine's performance until 20 per cent of its connections were gone. Moreover, if he retrained it after each destruction, he found it to be 80-per-cent accurate even with as much as 80 per cent of its connections destroyed. If 90 per cent of its connections were destroyed, it would still retain 70-per-cent accuracy. We have seen that a conventional computer, on the one hand, could not suffer anywhere near this kind of destruction and remain functional. On the other, the human brain loses the equivalent of Anderson's entire system every ten minutes and functions with near-perfect accuracy.

Although amazing, neural computers have their critics. Some AI researchers are more than a little distrustful of any appeal to the brain, because no one understands the connection between the brain and intelligence. Says Alfonso Caramazza, a cognitive psychologist at

Johns Hopkins, where NETtalk's Terry Sejnowski works, "Until someone can do that, it's just a lot of hogwash, because it creates an impression of understanding when there is deep ignorance."[12]

As we mentioned, the computer mentality is sympathetic to Caramazza's view, but at the same time it finds itself in an uncomfortable
position. It wants to separate intelligence from the brain; yet it can't
deny that Anderson's neural computer produces results that are almost indistinguishable from those of humans when it comes to pattern recognition. In this one respect, it has done a pretty fair job of
passing the Turing Test. But the Turing Test is one of the main
supports for the computer mentality's endeavor to convince us that
the conventional computer can embody intelligence just as well as the
brain. It is forced to swallow the evidence of the Turing Test for
neural computers, even though this goes against its basic assumption
that intelligence arises solely from symbol manipulation and not from
any particular neuronal properties, whether artificial or biological.

But neural computers make a lot of people uncomfortable. When
they hear of their abilities, almost invariably their response is: "That's
scary." These machines seem to stir something in the darker recesses
of our imaginations, perhaps in the same way that monsters in horror
stories and films do. Very often these monsters combine recognizable
human qualities along with something basically inhuman; so we are
both attracted and repulsed at the same time, confronted with something beyond our comprehension or control. What could be more
human than intelligence. and yet less human than glass, metal or
laser beams—something that is seemingly unconfined by time, space
or death?

Yet we must deal with our knowledge, even if it disturbs, disorients
or threatens us. We need not talk of monster computers to know that
intelligent machines are going to affect us psychologically, one way
or the other. So apart from these new neural machines and the fact
that artificial intelligence is still in its infancy, it is only natural to
wonder how computers are affecting us today.

5
ADJUSTING TO THE AGE OF THE COMPUTER

Computers are going to affect our thinking and shape our responses to everyday life. And though there is little documented information as to what this will look like, two important studies have been published, Craig Brod's *Technostress: The Human Cost of the Computer Revolution* and Sherry Turkle's *The Second Self: Computers and the Human Spirit.* Both these books deal with the effect of computers in the lives of both children and adults, but they differ in approach and emphasis.

Brod is interested in people's inability to cope with the new computer technologies and the disorders that result when the delicate balance between people and computers is upset—what he calls technostress. Although Turkle points out the dangers that computers hold for certain types of people, she is more interested in the role of computers in children's psychological development—for better or for worse. She is also interested in how computational ideas and meta-phors are moving from the narrow confines of the computer subculture into the culture at large and how computational language is displacing conventional psychological language in the way we think about ourselves. These books explain how the computer can affect our ability to sustain intimate personal relationships and how it enters into children's maturation.

Computers are not merely a matter of scientific, commercial or social concern. They touch us personally. They get inside us and shape our responses to life—for instance, it will probably seem natural for the next generation to accept the computer mentality's way of talking about life and what is important about being human. Although not everyone will accept the computer mentality's viewpoint, the danger exists that the terms or concepts people use to discuss these important issues will be defined or restricted by it. Let's see just how personal the computer can be.

The Personal Computer

Psychotherapist Craig Brod is concerned with the disorders that computers bring about in the emotions and minds of ordinary people—people who would not be considered abnormal by any of the usual psychological criteria. Brod's interest in technostress began with a patient, a seasoned computer programmer, who spoke of feeling let down and depleted; he especially complained of marital problems. His wife, he joked, made a terrible peripheral—technospeak for a subsidiary machine attached to the main computer, such as a printer or data storage unit.

At first Brod thought he was dealing with a classic workaholic, but after several months he found a cognitive pattern he couldn't explain. Slowly he understood that it wasn't his patient's past or personality type that was the source of the problem but the computer itself. Realizing that he had happened on a new phenomenon, Brod began three years of in-depth interviews, working first with adults and then with children from ages five to sixteen. Secretaries, executives, programmers and teen-agers, all at different levels and phases of computer adaptation, revealed the effects computers were having on their professional and personal lives. But most important were the effects on their personal relationships.[1]

Linda and Richard had been married for seven years. Richard had been a warm and emotional person—that is, before he became the director of computer services for a large bank. Once his computer skills and job responsibilities overtook his life, he didn't seem to need his circle of close friends anymore—or his wife. He no longer talked about anything except computers and had no patience with easygoing, informal conversation. He responded to factual exchanges or commands, such as "Wash the car" or "Do the dishes," but if Linda asked him "How do you feel about that?" he would retort, "What do you want from me?"

Says Linda: "He wasn't conversing. It was fact, fact—he was *facting!* Our entire conversation consisted of data. We exchanged random bits of unconnected information."

But it wasn't just conversation that made Richard impatient—so did life's normal tempos. One night, for example, when he and Linda were walking from a bus stop, she asked him to slow down a bit.

"Walk faster," he snapped.

"I can't walk faster," she protested, "my legs are shorter than yours."

"That's no excuse. You have to learn to walk more efficiently."

Linda grew tired of running and facting and eventually left Richard. "The only way I could have made the marriage work," she says, "is to have become floppy. You know, passive, totally floppy."

Joann, on the other hand, was a successful bank computer manager. As soon as she came home from work, she went into the bedroom and shut the door. Her only topic of conversation was computers. She had no energy for anything else. "Bad day?" her husband would ask. "Yup." "You want to talk about it?" "Nope"—and into the bedroom she went, shutting the door behind her. Home became a place to recover from work, a place to gather herself together just to survive. Any talk of family matters with her husband led to fights. Looking back on herself at that time she says, "The person who walked in that door after surviving ten hours with a dumb computer was not a nice person." Eventually, Joann quit her job. Her life began to change immediately:

I began to enjoy life. I enjoyed my home. I developed a real relationship with my husband. We decided we had a marriage after all. And I started to grow as a person. The entire nine years I managed that department, I wasn't developing. It's strange to begin to grow at thirty.

Jeremy is president of his own software company. Although he knows a great deal about computers, especially from the business side, he is not hooked on them. The technostress in his marriage came from his wife, Carol, a programmer. Jeremy became so jealous of Carol's addiction to the computer that on more than one occasion he smashed her computer in a rage. The next day Carol would buy another. He would feel sorry after his violent outburst, he says, "but having to experience her as half-computer . . . is just as bad." Even if he could get her to leave the computer and sit with him, watch TV or just read the paper together, her mind would still be on the computer. All of a sudden she would say, "I've got it! If I just take the I/O board and . . ."

This situation, indeed the very words Carol uses, is almost identical to a long-running television ad campaign intended to show the creativity and dedication of the systems team in a particular computer firm. We are shown a preoccupied young woman going home with something on her mind. Suddenly in the middle of the night she sits bolt upright in bed and says, "That's it!" We see her rush down the hall, jump over the janitor's vacuum cleaner, burst into the conference room and announce something like, "If we process the whatchemajigs first and then . . ." The most striking difference between the make-believe programmers in this series of ads and Carol is that we never see any spouses in the ads—a complication that the copy writers neatly avoid.

Once Carol had a dream in which she actually became her computer. She visited its insides going from I/O board to I/O board. The next day she had a tremendous insight into the problem she was working on, and she felt much closer to her machine. Says Jeremy, "I felt I was sharing her with the computer, barely. Most of the time I got nothing, and the computer got everything." When their psychotherapist tried to break through, she would say, "I can't talk about this—I feel like my head is going to implode," or, "I have an inability to process data on this level"—all of which is another way of saying, "Sorry, this doesn't compute."

Carol quit her programming job. Jeremy says, "Since quitting her job, Carol's changing. I find a new Carol now—more loving, more sensuous, more of a human being. Before she quit, I was only getting about two per cent of the human part of her."

Ron and Alice have been married eighteen years and for the past fifteen years Ron has handled the computer payroll system for a large department in a city government. Aside from the usual pressures, like having to cancel vacations and getting phone calls in the night, Alice finds the most difficult thing to endure is Ron's completely analytic outlook on life. If she pours out her feelings about a problem, he coldly considers the facts of the situation and presents the solution. "But a lot of times you don't want a solution," says Alice. "You just need someone to say that it's going to be okay, you'll be all right." Ron can't relax; he sits in front of the television and falls asleep while talking about his work. Like Carol, he wakes up in the middle of the night with the answer to a problem he has been dreaming about— an advertiser's delight.

Arnold is a manager of a corporate data-processing department and, like Jeremy, is able to maintain a balance between his work and home life. The trouble began when he suggested that Kay, his wife, buy a home computer to practice programming to help her with her new job as assistant to a systems analyst. Kay began to change as she became more and more involved with the machine. She had little time or energy for him and quickly became impatient when they tried to talk. One night in bed she turned to him and asked, "Are you on-line tonight or not?" Although she is doing well at work, their marriage is in deep trouble.

Janet, a systems analyst, plans to have sex with her husband several days in advance in order to fit it into her schedule so as not to disrupt her involvement with the computer. She has lost contact with herself as a sexual being and has no desire for her husband. Sex is not a part of her total being nor a loving bond between them; rather, it is a way of releasing tension and not much else.

Jay's fiancée accompanied him when he took his first programming job after graduating from college. Nine months later they broke up. His fiancée had too many expectations of him. "I didn't have time for romance anymore. It was time to grow up, and I couldn't spend all that time 'relating' and everything we did in college." Nowadays he describes his relationships with women as "efficient." The women with whom he has relations are computer workers like himself, and he views these women as quite interchangeable with one another.

Men, Women and Computers

Sex and computers seem to be competitors for our natural energy. When the computer takes over, technocentered victims can't feel what their needs are or even if they have needs. Brod finds that sexuality is not so much repressed as it is controlled. Sexual desire is unpredictable and spontaneous; it is directly opposed to the planning and control functions of the technocentered individual. The real source of immediacy, excitement and power for the technocentered individual, says Brod, is technical mastery, which offers the illusion of protection from life's vicissitudes. The technocentered individual feels that she or he can rise above the needs and vulnerabilities of mere mortals and achieve a measure of omnipotence. The result, ironically, is loneliness, increased vulnerability and lack of sexual responsiveness.

The computer is no respecter of gender when it comes to threatening a person's ability to lovingly relate to others. But Brod found, as did Turkle, that women tend to break away from the computer's holding power more readily than men when the dangers are perceived. Moreover, Brod reports that although women married to technocentered men were unhappy, they didn't often contemplate divorce or infidelity but regarded their mate's behavior as an exaggeration of a normal situation. Men, on the other hand, expressed much greater anger and jealousy toward their technocentered wives, feeling that their mate's behavior was a considerable aberration. Nevertheless, Brod writes, because the computer reaches so deeply into the psyche, it recognizes no sex-role differences.

Brod summarizes the characteristics he has found among people who have overidentified with the computer: an unusually high degree of factual thinking, an inability to feel, an insistence on efficiency and speed, a lack of empathy for others, an intolerance for the ambiguities of human behavior and communication, and a lessening of their ability to think intuitively and creatively. Along with the technocentered individual's disdain of ambiguity is an obsession for order and predictability. If the coffee cup is not in its right place, he becomes disgruntled because misplaced things are a violation of the rules, an interruption in the orderly progression of the morning's agenda or program. Memories of the past and hopes for the future are severely curtailed. The ability to experience life to the full has disappeared.

There is hope for many technocentered individuals. Often when they leave computer work or reorganize their lives to break the cycle of machine dependence, they become new people, or the people they once were before becoming involved with the computer. They become empathic and affectionate, unlike the obsessive-compulsive people they once resembled. Obsessive-compulsive people, unlike those suffering from technostress, says Brod, remain driven in any situation; if they break off from their work, they will become just as compulsive about gardening, carpentry, jogging or anything else they take up.

As we mentioned, Brod also interviewed children and teen-agers and found, not surprisingly, widespread symptoms of technostress. "More machinelike than childlike," he says, "these children seek isolation from family members, view others as highly inefficient, and experience traditional learning activities like reading as painfully slow. They have been socialized by the computer."[2] These children suffer from the same mental strain, alteration of time, tyranny of perfection, mechanical social relations and isolation that technostressed adults experience. In general, he says, there is a reduction of external sensory experience so that the real world fades, and children are locked in the world of the machine. Here they become accustomed to a rapid-fire dialog with the machine so that in one sense time speeds up, and in another sense it becomes nonexistent. Switching between the computer world and the real world becomes a problem. As one thirteen-year-old puts it: "Work with the computer is like being in a bubble. Once my bubble's broken all the liquid flops out, and then I can be outside again. I shake once or twice, and I'm back in the real world again, trying to function like normal."[3]

We must keep in mind that Brod is looking at children and adults who are already feeling the harmful effects of the computer, but not all people are going to be affected in such a manner. Turkle's study, on the other hand, is much broader; she is trying to determine how the computer enters our psychological development in healthy as well as unhealthy ways. Not all her subjects are suffering from emotional disorders.

Turkle's Children

Turkle used more than two hundred children and two hundred adults in her study—and she did more than just interview them. She sat in elementary classrooms where computers were being used. She played with computer toys along with young children, sometimes asking questions, sometimes just listening; she recorded snatches of conversations of college students in halls and laboratories and taped long soliloquies in which people expressed their innermost thoughts and feelings about computers and themselves.

You can't read this important work without being amazed by the kinds of questions the computer raises in the minds of those who use them, especially very young children. What stands out is that the computer causes children to think profound thoughts about life, people, themselves and God—thoughts that most of us get secondhand in college-level courses in philosophy, psychology or religion. Something else comes across quite clearly—these thoughts are not a veneer. They are not mere niceties as they would be for many of us, demonstrating that we are acquainted with some of the great issues of Western thought or that we are well-rounded, well-educated people. They arise naturally and spontaneously in the minds of children and seem to have nothing to do with teachers, course outlines or the adult world—and these issues most certainly enter into children's mental and emotional development.

Turkle is often asked, "Are computers good or bad—especially for children?" No one, she observes, asks in the same broad, philosophical sense whether our relationships with people are good or bad. We try to build our own model of a particular relationship with another person and then make judgments about its effects on us, but only now are we beginning to think in this way about our relationships with technology. "Computers are not good or bad," she asserts, "they are powerful." When we think about the power of computers, however, it is usually in the context of their objective, instrumental use. Turkle directs our attention to their subjective side, their second nature, their power to fascinate and disturb, to evoke strong feelings or precipitate thoughts. "If the reader is surprised by the intensity or the range of responses I report," she adds, "this is only to the good if it leads to a critical reexamination of what each of us takes for granted about 'The Computer' and to an attitude of healthy skepticism toward any who propose simple scenarios about the 'impact of the computer on society.' "[4]

But Turkle's study is unsettling even to those who *have* thought about the effect of computers. It isn't just an out-of-the-mouths-of-babes situation where we condescendingly chuckle and go on our way. There is nothing infantile about a four-year-old thinking that a computer is alive when, as we shall see, influential books have been written asserting that they are. In case after case, Turkle shows that all the issues surrounding computers, AI and the computer mentality are not the idle academic speculations of a few specialists; they are of intense concern to our children and undoubtedly prefigure the future of society as a whole. The unnerving thing is that almost none of us has been aware that this is happening.

A point she makes repeatedly is that we cannot look for a single, universal effect of computers on the minds and emotions of children—the sort of effect, for example, that television supposedly has in turning viewers into passive zombies. Different children react to computers in different ways. Nevertheless, Turkle has identified three stages children go through in their relationship with the computer. She calls the first stage, when children are roughly four to seven years old, "metaphysical." Children want to know whether the machine can think, if it can feel and, above all, if it is alive. The second stage, from age seven or eight to adolescence, is the "mastery" stage, when children are interested in using the computer as a means of growing competent, of exploring their effectiveness in the world. In the third stage, "identity," adolescents use the machine as a way of thinking about themselves, of self-discovery. The three stages can be summarized by the types of questions children ask: What is this thing? What can I do with it? and Who am I?

What Is This Thing?

What is so important about the metaphysical stage, that period of our lives when we classify objects into categories of the living and the nonliving? Psychologists suggest that we form theories about the objects around us in order to dispel our fear of them. If we are able to talk about them and classify them, they are less scary; we neutralize their threat and gain a measure of control. When children build theories about what is or isn't alive, they use everything around them—flowers, dogs, people, the sun, wind-up toys—but most of all they use what they know best: themselves. This is the root of childhood animism: stones roll or the sun moves because they "want to," because that's what children would do. As children grow older, such physical notions as wheels, levers or gravity come to replace personal, psychological ones. Later on, about the age of eleven or so, biological notions, such as growth, breathing or eating, help children to divide the world into the living and the nonliving. Psychological notions come to be associated with people or animals.

Turkle's study shows that computers disturb this orderly progression. Children are not sure how to classify computer toys that talk, teach and win at games—objects that respond and interact in ways that are often far more psychologically sophisticated than those of dogs, cats or sunfish. The computer upsets neat divisions because it is a marginal object—it is a thing and yet it has a piece of a mind within it. Part of the difficulty the computer poses for children, indeed for many adults as well, is its physical opacity—we can't see any levers or cogs or anything else to account for its actions. Nor can it be explained in any of the physical concepts children have so carefully constructed to account for the vast nonliving portion of the world; still, it doesn't eat, grow or have babies either. Children have no recourse other than to think of it in terms of the mind: Is it conscious? Does it have feelings? Does it play fair? Does it cheat?

Turkle's study makes it abundantly clear, however, that this is not like ordinary childhood animism. She found that although infantile animism is superseded by physical criteria (which in turn is superseded by biological criteria in the case of noncomputational objects), when it comes to the aliveness of computers and computer toys, psychological notions dominate from the earliest years and become even more pronounced and subtler as children grow older. This comes as a revelation to those who think it should be obvious to anyone, especially for children over twelve, that any discussion of computer aliveness should be ruled out for the simple reason that computers are not biological.

Of course the more important question is not whether children think the computer is alive, but how the computer enters into the development of their ideas of mind or, as Turkle puts it, the construction of the psychological. The following gives a flavor of how the psychological enters the question of aliveness. Here are some comments from children about Speak and Spell, a widely available computer toy.[5]

A four-year-old says it's alive because "it has a talking voice in it."

A five-year-old says: "It's alive—it talks."

An eight-year-old confidently proclaims: "Things that talk are alive."

A six-year-old concludes, after closely examining Speak and Spell: "It's alive—there's a man inside of it."

Eight-year-old Adam overhears five-year-old Lucy say that it's alive because it talks. "OK, so it talks," he says, "but it's not really thinking of what it's saying. It's not alive."

Here we have a conventional argument that many of us would give to put at rest the whole notion of computer life or intelligence. But Lucy (five, remember) comes back with: "You can't talk if you don't think, Adam. That's why babies can't talk. They don't know how to think good enough yet." And here we have the standard AI reply to such an argument: computers just aren't smart enough yet, but when they are. . . .

What is startling about such comments (quite typical, by the way) is that children use psychological concepts to argue both sides of the issue, and not physical or biological ones. Turkle reports that in addition to talking and consciousness, the most common psychological attributes children use in discussing the computer's aliveness are intelligence, feeling and morality. When Turkle asked children in a computer-rich elementary classroom "Are computers alive?" the most frequent answer she received was an ambivalent "Sort of." Computers think but don't feel; they learn but don't decide what to learn; they cheat but don't know they are cheating. For computer-smart children there are no simple answers, and their responses reflect a skill and discernment in using psychological concepts that their parents never needed at that age.

That biology is irrelevant for arguing computer aliveness is not the only surprise; consciousness is not all that important, either. For most of us, the idea of consciousness grows along with our idea of life itself. When we think about objects in biological terms, we ascribe consciousness only to people or animals. The idea that computers couldn't possibly have a sense of consciousness because they aren't alive has a lot of force for us adults. Not so for many children, who will allow a computer to have consciousness long after denying it life. For them, something can be conscious, even have malicious intentions, and not be completely alive. From preschool on up, computers are reorienting children's view that human life is irrevocably intertwined with biology and consciousness. The next question, then, is "What makes humans so special?"

Since children perceive machines to be smart, if not smarter than they, intelligence—the traditional answer to the question—cannot be what makes us unique. The answer for children, Turkle says, is becoming less dependent on intellect and more dependent on feelings and emotions. In a study of eighty-eight children ranging from four to eleven, Turkle reports that almost 90 per cent of the children over eight said that the difference between computers and people is that people have feelings. "Computers are smart, but they don't have feelings" or "Computers are good at games and puzzles and math, but they could never have emotions."[6] On the other hand, an eight-year-old said, "You can have a computer or robot that has feelings, but it's not alive. You have to program it, you have to put in this special 'feelings cassette.' "[7] In a later chapter we will see just how close this remark is to the views and hopes of certain AI researchers.

On the one hand, children grant that machines are intelligent and capable of many human mental states, while on the other, they don't grant them the ability to love or hate. This ambiguity presents a danger. When children begin to define themselves in opposition to the machine solely on the basis of emotion, the complex relationships between thought and feeling are torn asunder, with the result being that they view themselves not as rational animals but as "emotional machines," as Turkle puts it. When the computer drives a wedge into our intellectual sensibilities, thought splits off on the side of logical procedure and analytical thinking, while emotion falls on the side of the primal, the uncontrollable and the unanalyzable.

Technostress will only become more and more commonplace as people grow up thinking of themselves and others as machines to be manipulated or exploited—an ironic situation for those who distinguish themselves from machines on the basis of feeling. Turkle sees a danger that people who think of themselves as emotional machines will come to regard the delicate balance between thought and feeling in a shallow or sentimental light. She is concerned about a generation that takes "the mix of mysticism, Zen, and romanticism that is the message of Yoda and the Force as what distinguishes the human in the world of robots."[8]

The difference between thought and emotion is not the only criterion that children use to come to grips with the computer's aliveness and otherness. Although morality—doing what one ought to do—is not something children normally use to determine what is alive or not, it came up with surprising frequency in Turkle's study, especially in the area of cheating.

The connection between aliveness and cheating was most evident when children encountered Merlin, a computer toy that plays tic-tac-toe. Merlin is programmed to follow a strategy that at worst enables it to draw; that is, either it wins (if children make mistakes) or it draws (if they make no mistakes). It is also programmed to depart from this strategy every so often so that children have the opportunity to win occasionally. But when children try in subsequent games to repeat their winning moves, they can do no better than draw, because Merlin is once more following its no-lose procedure. Yet machines are supposed to be predictable; what they do one time, they are supposed to do all the time. Merlin surprises children by doing what it ought not to do. Therefore, they conclude, Merlin must be cheating. Moreover, when children win by watching out for Merlin's lapse, they believe they are, in turn, cheating Merlin. Turkle records a delightful scene of a small group of young children discussing Merlin's moral rectitude.[9]

Robert, seven, after trying the supposed winning trick, throws Merlin down on the ground in frustration: "Cheater. I hope your brains break." Greg, eight, replies: "Someone taught Merlin to play. But he doesn't know if he wins or loses."

Robert: "Yes, he does know if he loses. He makes different noises."

Greg: "No, stupid. It's smart. It's smart enough to make the right kinds of noises. But it doesn't really know if it loses. That's how you can cheat it. It doesn't know you are cheating. And when it cheats, it doesn't even know it's cheating."

Jenny, six, jumps in the conversation with a disdainful rejoinder: "Greg, to cheat you have to know you are cheating. Knowing is part of cheating."

On the surface it would appear that Jenny's argument should support Greg's instead of rebutting it as she intends. But beneath all three children's arguments is the assumption that Merlin does indeed cheat, and for both Robert and Jenny there is another assumption underlying that: knowing is part of cheating. In Jenny's thinking, Greg is making a logical error.

In this brief encounter we catch a glimpse of how computational or technological concepts can shape our philosophical and psychological outlook from our earliest years. Although we may deny the idea of computer life, feeling or intentionality, our actions may belie our thoughts. The important point here is not whether children think computers are alive or not, or whether computers will ever become as intelligent as humans, but the nature of the discourse, the kind of thinking that computers evoke, especially as it enters the way we think of ourselves. Millions of parents, says Turkle, buy computers or computer toys with the hope of giving their children the edge in spelling, math or hand-eye coordination. What parents don't recognize is that in the hands of children, such objects "become the occasion for theorizing, for fantasizing, for thinking through metaphysically charged questions to which childhood searches for a response."[10]

What Can I Do with It?

But how do computers enter into children's psychological development as they grow older, moving into the mastery stage? Although each child is affected differently and to a different degree, Turkle discovered something about the quality of the interaction between children and computers and how computers modify the way children from ages eight to eleven begin to discover and develop their sense of competence in the world. She found that they divided into two main personality groups: hard masters and soft masters.

Hard masters want to impose their will over the machine by using logic to bring order to chaos, precision to imprecision, and certainty to uncertainty; they also enjoy interacting with something that resists or fights back. Soft masters see the computer as something to be negotiated with, responded to and psychologized; their approach is more verbal, visual, almost sensual, in contrast to the hard master's detached and abstract approach.

Although hard masters fit our stereotype of the kind of people who are attracted to computers, Turkle's study provides ample evidence that computers attract soft masters as well—and this doesn't fit our stereotype. We usually think of the computer as imposing its internal, logical procedures and structures on the user, but modern interactive computer systems allow for the reverse; that is, the computer conforms to the shape of children's imagination so that it becomes a way of dealing with the world, coping with problems and resolving conflicts. The computer becomes an expression and amplifier of children's personalities while maintaining its otherness in their minds. It becomes, as Turkle's book indicates, a second self.

Turkle has many examples of soft masters negotiating with this second self, but this is our favorite.[11] Tanya was a black fifth grader who couldn't spell or write but who had an intense interest in spoken words, especially the language of the Bible. "I go by the word of the Lord, the word of the Bible," she would say. "If you have the deep-down Holy Ghost and you are speaking in the tongue which God has spoke through you, you hearken to the word." The words would pour out in a great rhythmic flow, passionate and compelling, nothing like the language in her textbooks and readers. "School is not a good place for my kind of words," she said.

In Tanya we see a personality who should be as antipathetic to the computer as anyone we can imagine. When she first met the computer at the beginning of the sixth grade, she thought of it as some sort of little toy animal that could talk. To no avail she tried to make it respond by talking with it and then shouting at it, calling it a fool. She finally used the keyboard as she had been instructed and was able to give the computer a name—Peter. That was the beginning. The first one in and the last one out during computer periods, she began writing a torrent of letters and stories about everybody she knew, including people she had been afraid to speak to and to whom she gave her letters as a first act of friendship.

She introduced Peter to visitors and signed all her computer stories with "Peter and Tanya." She flew in a rage when her teachers insisted that all computers were identical. He was special, different, more than a thing—and he was very close: "When you are with a computer, you know the whole time what you are saying. You have it inside your ear. When you are using your fingers to be with Peter, [you are] using emotions with the computer."

Two years later Tanya's relationship with Peter wasn't what it once was; she is her own person and thinks of herself as a writer, a poet. When she graduated from middle school, the school library accepted her gift of a volume of her poems. For Tanya the computer was a means of developing and releasing what was already in her; it enabled her to break out of her isolation and relate to a larger culture, quite the opposite of how most of us think the computer affects people.

Soft masters are indeed masters; the complexities of machine interaction have become second nature for them. The difference between
the hards and softs is illustrated in the way children identify with the
elements in the programs they construct. When a hard master identifies with an abstraction, he may put himself in its place in a program
but only in order to figure out how to command its actions. A soft
master, on the other hand, will take her whole personality, everything
she thinks she is, into a world she feels is populated not with abstractions but with peoplelike entities.

Our choice of pronouns in these last two sentences is intentional.
Although both boys and girls can be soft masters, it is rare to find girls
who are hard masters. This fact is noted by all commentators of
computer culture. Those children, almost exclusively boys, who carry
hard mastery into adulthood to its extreme, obsessive form are called
"hackers." Hackers have been observed, discussed and written about
for years. Anyone in a computer environment even for a short time
can spot them immediately. But no one has described them better
than Joseph Weizenbaum, a pioneer in artificial intelligence and one
of its most astute critics:

> Wherever computer centers have become established, that is to say,
> in countless places in the United States, as well as in virtually all
> other industrial regions of the world, bright young men of dishev-
> eled appearance, often with sunken glowing eyes, can be seen
> sitting at computer consoles, their arms tensed and waiting to fire
> their fingers, already poised to strike, at the buttons and keys on
> which their attention seems to be riveted as a gambler's on the
> rolling dice. When not so transfixed, they often sit at tables strewn
> with computer printouts over which they pore like possessed stu-
> dents of a cabalistic text.[12]

Hackers like to have their food, mostly junk food, brought to them;
they sleep in cots beside the computer, their clothes are rumpled, their
bodies unwashed, their hair uncombed, their faces unshaven. They
live for one thing only—the computer.

But seldom do we find female hackers. Although Turkle found a
few girls addicted to computer video games—and girl soft masters
certainly become as involved with computers as hard masters—girls,

she says, try to forge relationships with the computer that bypass objectivity altogether. They don't regard the computer's formal procedures as a set of hard and fast rules to which the microworld must conform but rather as a language for communicating and negotiating with a psychological other. Male hard masters, on the other hand, tend to use the computers as a way of controlling a world, a way of acting out a fantasy. As Weizenbaum observes: "No playwright, no stage director, no emperor, however powerful, has ever exercised such absolute authority to arrange a stage or a field of battle and to command such unswervingly dutiful actors or troops."[13] But even when control is an issue with a girl, it is not usually control over something external but a matter of self-control—control over her temper, eating or smoking. Moreover, Turkle found, as did Brod with adults, that when girls begin to sense that the machine is controlling them, they withdraw from it. Not so with boys; adolescent males face a danger of getting stuck—and not just during their young adulthood.

Who Am I?

This phenomenon of computers and gender leads us to the last stage—the period of adolescence when the question of identity becomes paramount. The computer affords teen-agers an opportunity to think about themselves and learn who they are. Adolescents spend hours in front of the mirror, fascinated by their fast-changing bodies, trying to see how they must appear to other people. Similarly, the computer serves as a mind-mirror—it allows them to see their inner selves from the outside. The following remarks are typical of the young adolescents in Turkle's study. An eighth-grade boy said, "I could see what I was doing on the computer, and I could see what a nut I was." A thirteen-year-old girl said, "When you program a computer, there is a little piece of your mind, and now it's a little piece of the computer's mind . . . and now you can see it."[14] You can program it to be just like you, she goes on. You can give it your thoughts, your feelings; you can see the things inside yourself and change them around.

In case after case, Turkle shows how adolescents use the computer as a means of objectifying their whole approach to life and working through personal concerns. They do this in two ways: they project themselves into the computer, and they develop their thoughts about who they are by comparing themselves to the computer's internal structures. Just as the language of psychoanalysis provides metaphors for thinking about oneself, the computer also provides a set of concepts, a computational language, for self-reference. The difference is that no one teaches children the metaphors of computation—they formulate them early in childhood through direct experience. Moreover, there is a difference between psychoanalytic and computational metaphors in that computational metaphors are more allegorical in nature. Children are able to make one-to-one comparisons between the computer and themselves because the computer is enough like a mind to enable them to manipulate complex, partially understood feelings and thoughts in objective, precise patterns on the machine.

Some children, especially as they grow older, use computational concepts explicitly in thinking about themselves. Turkle reports that fourteen-year-old Dennis, for example, identifies the inner core of himself with the computer's low-level machine language, whereas his personality is like the computer's high-level languages. Dennis is continually preoccupied with how he is both like and unlike his father. He sees his father as intellectual, intense and successful, and he tries to shape his own identity distinct from his father's but somehow close to it. Using the image that he and his father have two different machine language cores, like those of an IBM or a DEC, he has decided that they are quite different in a fundamental way. But all the things he likes about his father, as well as those he doesn't, he can either accommodate or bypass in his high-level language self. And what doesn't come out right can always be reprogrammed.

The idea that the self is a program occurs with some frequency not only among adolescents but young children and adults as well. Recall Carla, the girl we mentioned at the beginning of the book, who had an answer to the argument that computers aren't alive because they are programmed. "Well, I don't know if they are alive. They are certainly not completely alive, but I don't think it has to do with that they're programmed. We are all programmed."[15] This is not a depressing thought for either Dennis or Carla. They don't think of themselves as automatons driven by a set of inexorable rules. Furthermore, there is always the hope that their programs—who they are—can be reprogrammed.

Who Is Everyone Else?

Some teen-agers seek their identity in what the computer is, while others define themselves in opposition to it. Some use it to see themselves like others; some use it to see themselves as apart or different from others. For some, the computer helps in their socialization process; for others, it provides an escape from the uncertain world of emotions and human relationships. Here many adolescents, especially boys, get in trouble with the computer, and it almost always is linked to a deep-seated need to control their lives. Computers become a sanctuary in a world of highly charged and unpredictable feelings.

The computer can be a positive influence in a child's growth and development, especially in fostering a sense of worth and efficacy through the mastery of computational intricacies. But a computer also affords a kind of companionship without the threats of human intimacy. Increasingly, a child reaches out to others through the machine, and this doesn't cease with childhood.

Turkle talks of Alex, a college student who sometimes spends up to fifteen hours a day on the computer. He loves sending electronic mail via the computer to people all over the country—so much so that he sometimes thinks that is more of an addiction than the computer itself. Says Alex:

I would say that I have a perfect interface with the machine . . . perfect for me. I feel totally telepathic with the computer. And it sort of generalizes so that I feel telepathic with the people I am sending mail to. I am glad I don't have to see them face to face. I wouldn't be as personal about myself. And the telepathy with the computer—well, I certainly don't think of it as a person there, but that doesn't mean that I don't *feel* it as a person there. Particularly since I have so personalized my interface with the system to suit myself. So it's like being with another person, but not a strange

person. Someone who knows just how I like things done.[16]
Instead of learning how to negotiate in the give-and-take world of human relationships, a child can become so immersed in a microworld over which he has complete control that he comes to see himself in relation to others in two extremes: either he controls them or they control him. This dichotomy becomes more pronounced as children move through their teens and into young adulthood, especially when it comes to sex and romance. Anthony, a twenty-year-old senior at MIT, puts it this way:

> [Hackers] are used to having this very close, clear, intimate relationship with the computer and they expect to have the same kind of relationship with a girl. They expect to understand the other person more than it is possible; they expect more control over the other person than is reasonable. People just don't work like computers.[17]

If we hadn't seen it already in Brod's subjects, it might surprise us that an object of logic and formal procedures, a mind machine, could have anything to do with sexuality. After all, computers are not like guns or fancy racing cars—machines that some observers have associated with sexual thrills. But the common strain seems to be the excitement that arises from the delicate, almost exquisite, interplay between having control and losing it. Turkle reports that MIT hackers liken this kind of play to "sport death," pushing themselves and the machine to the limits, pushing the system to the point of technical failure so that only by having the right stuff can they save the situation. How far can they go? How much can they get away with? Winning and domination are everything—more important than school, people or their own bodies.

Is it hard to imagine all this sublimated sex and violence going on in the mind of a young man sitting transfixed in front of a screen, with the only sound the quiet clicking of the keyboard? Maybe, until we recognize the computer's holding power, how it conveys a sense of being alive and how it can replace normal human relationships. Now imagine this same person, older, sitting at the console of the most advanced computer weapons systems in the world and playing a game where life and death are not merely in his mind.

80116

Enter the Computer Mentality

One of the reasons we have not mentioned the computer mentality thus far is that it is not a psychological disorder but rather a philosophical one. It may be true that someone who has the computer mentality is isolated from life, unable to sustain intimate relationships or obsessed by the desire for control, but these do not characterize the computer mentality. The computer mentality is not so much a victim of the computer as it is an aggressive world view that sees people and computers as manifestations of information processing. There is a reciprocal relationship between the computer mentality and what we saw happening in the psyches of adults and children: the computer mentality will foster and support the ways the computer enters into our psychological development; in turn, the computer mentality's world view will be more readily accepted by those whose thinking has been shaped by the computer.

Children already think of the computer as "sort of alive" without reference to biology. Nor is biology necessary for consciousness in their minds—something their parents would find inconceivable. Joseph Weizenbaum says much the same thing:

I accept the idea that a computer system is sufficiently complex and autonomous to warrant our talking about it as an organism. Given that it can both sense and affect its environment, I even grant that it can, in an extremely limited sense, be 'socialized,' that is, modified by its experiences with its world. I grant also that a suitably constructed robot can be made to develop a sense of itself, that it can, for example, learn to distinguish between parts of itself and objects outside of itself, that it can be made to assign higher priority to guarding its own parts against physical damage than to similarly guarding objects external to itself, and that it can form a model of itself which could, in some sense, be considered a kind of self-consciousness. When I say therefore that I am willing to regard such a robot as an 'organism,' I declare my willingness to consider it a kind of animal. And . . . I see no way to put a bound on the degree of intelligence such an organism could, at least in principle, attain.[18]

Although Weizenbaum doesn't come right out and say that a computer is alive, he comes pretty close when he uses words like "organism," "animal" and "self-conscious." Clearly he is saying, along with Turkle's children, that the computer is sort of alive. But what is life—at least in a technical sense? Even though no one doubts that we ourselves are alive, as are animals and trees and bacteria, a comprehensive answer is not so simple. How does the computer mentality argue from the sort-of-alive position to asserting that computers are a life form? And why does it wish to do so?

In his book *Are Computers Alive? Evolution and New Life Forms,* Geoff Simons, chief editor of England's National Computing Centre, claims that computers are at least as alive, if not more so, than a virus, which is one of those problematic, sort-of-alive things. The difficulty is that as scientists descend the ladder of living beings, they find it increasingly awkward to come up with a list of criteria that covers all life forms. The cell is the last rung that gives stable support, the last unquestionably living entity. Yet, does the ladder go down one more rung to the virus?

Everyone knows firsthand about a virus. But what is it? A virus is chemically similar to simple organisms that no one questions are alive. It consists of sugars, nitrogen bases and phosphates, all wrapped in a protective coat of protein. These same chemicals also make up the virus's strands of DNA, which stores its genetic information, or RNA, which normally translates the genetic message of its DNA into the building of protein, the stuff of life. In this regard it seems that a virus has some impressive qualifications for life. But it also has some major drawbacks.

A virus has no enzymes that enable it to assimilate food; it can't generate its own metabolic energy necessary for its maintenance, growth or reproduction. So how is it that we keep getting runny noses and hacking coughs? By cunning and subterfuge. A virus invades a living cell and, in effect, substitutes its own genetic machinery in place of the cell's. The unwitting cell dutifully follows the bogus instructions, replicating over and over again the virus instead of itself, until it bursts. The new-made viruses escape and drift off to redo the whole destructive business in fresh hosts. So even though a virus can't do for itself what a cell can do, it can take on traits we usually associate with life. But there is something else that makes it suspect for life status.

Let's look at the example of one of the most thoroughly studied viruses—the tobacco mosaic virus (TMV) that infects the leaves of tobacco plants. When its fortunes reverse and it can't find any living cells to sponge off, TMV hibernates, in a sense. But unlike bears, which continue breathing and looking like bears all winter long, TMV becomes a needlelike crystal, inert and, to all appearances, lifeless. But when it is dissolved in water, it reactivates and begins infecting tobacco leaves with its old vigor. A complex computer system is remarkably similar to a virus like TMV, says Simons.

A virus is a highly compact, at times mobile, information storage system, and not much else. In its crystalline form, a virus is not much different from a submicroscopic computer diskette. As a diskette needs a computer to activate its program, so a virus needs the machinery of a living cell to run its program. The essence of both a virus and a computer program is a nonphysical, logical structure—a code. Each code must be written in some kind of physical form—nucleic acid, on the one hand, and magnetic dots on the other—but each is mere potentiality until something sets it in motion.

Moreover, says Simons, a computer satisfies even more life criteria than a virus. In contrast to a virus, a computer can process energy in order to function; that is, it feeds on electrical energy and excretes heat as a waste product, an impossibility for a virus. Furthermore, a computer can reproduce itself in a matter of seconds each time it processes the COPY command in its list of instructions. Of course it takes a great deal longer to make its transistors, chips, boards and casing. And humans are needed to make all this, both the software and hardware, though computers are involved in their own reproduction from chip design to assembly. Nevertheless, listen to what David Ritchie says in his book *The Binary Brain: Artificial Intelligence in the Age of Electronics:*

> It is not too outlandish to speculate that perhaps we are the computers' reproductive system. We may serve the computers in much the same manner that ovaries and testicles serve humans, as mechanisms for keeping the species in business.[19]

Although Simons has other arguments for claiming that computers deserve life status, he reminds us that a living computer need not be as sophisticated a life form as a dog or a human. For him, computers are a rudimentary form of life, and they meet the criteria we expect to find in the biological world from the paramecium to humankind. Yet it is difficult to take Simons's argument seriously. A computer is manmade, and no one has ever claimed that an artifact is alive, even if we do kick and yell at our cars when they don't start. It isn't clear, for example, how we would distinguish a living machine from a non-living machine using his life criteria. Nor is a computer made out of hydrocarbons, the stuff of life. Nor does a computer die; we can always replace worn-out parts. We can't do that for plants or animals; there is a time, a season, when all living things must bow to the inevitable.

But Turkle's children bypassed these biological considerations when talking about computer aliveness—not that they aren't aware of the difference between flesh and metal. We might try to convince them that a computer is as far from being alive as a stone is from a tree, though we might not make much of an impression. Quite simply, they are looking at things from a different viewpoint—a psychological one.

Biologists have always had a set of criteria for determining aliveness, which are often abstract and far removed from what most of us use when thinking about life. What is so disturbing, then, about the computer mentality's using criteria based on information processing? Does it really matter? A biologist's definition is restricted and doesn't change the way any of us look at life in its broader manifestations. Whether a virus is alive doesn't have any bearing on what we make of our existence. But this is not the case when the computer mentality convinces people that computers are a life form. Here is the first step in redefining what is most important about who we are and what life means to us. The computer mentality's world view comprises our minds and our intelligence—and it does so apart from our biological constitution. It attempts to sever everything important about us from our creatureliness—and from the fact that we have been created by God. The computer mentality's desire to remove life from our very bodies is part of the same agenda that seeks to take intelligence and understanding from our brains. Its intent is clear: to make the rough places smooth, to prepare the way for the coming of the first man-made, inorganic species of life on earth—*machina sapiens*.

6
REDEFINING
OURSELVES

It is no surprise that computers are causing a revolution, not only in business and science, but in thinking—and in thinking about thinking, the field of cognitive psychology. Indeed, many of the foremost thinkers in computer science and artificial intelligence are not mathematicians or engineers but psychologists. These people are taking the ideas of how computers and programs work and applying them to how people and the mind work. We have seen that computers and programs are supposed to create intelligence by the interaction of millions of nonintelligent parts. And we have seen that in some ways we can accurately describe the function of the brain in a similar fashion: insentient neurons act and react through chemical stimuli that, added together, not only run our bodies but equip us to reason, imagine, invent.

How can we define humankind in the computer age? Humanity has been considered many things: clay, a rational animal, a clock. Now we are asking if it is also some sort of feeling computer. Or, to turn the situation around, certain thinkers are asking us to accept the computer as another kind of person. Will the terms be interchangeable? Computers not only affect the way we think and the way we think about thinking, but they affect our language—in short, our definition of humankind. We discuss our brain's input and output, its hardware and software; linguists deal with our language as if it were computer code; computers are said to think. How we define humanness in part determines how we define our role in nature and ultimately how we define God, for it is in the relationship between ourselves and him—only possible because of the right definitions—that we can understand our world at all.

Marvin Minsky of MIT, in his book *The Society of Mind,* offers the clearest, most comprehensive outline of the new definition of humankind we have seen. His views are already threatening to replace those of Freud, Jung, Rogers, Piaget and others. Unconsciously, Christians have appropriated much from these older psychologists, whether their views meshed with Christianity or not. With Minsky we have the opportunity to consider what is to come before it becomes as common in our thinking as id, libido or collective unconscious.

Minsky has coined the phrase *society of mind* to describe the mental life of a human being. This inner social structure of our mind comprises millions of small processes he calls agents, each of which can do only one simple, specialized thing that requires no intelligence at all. Yet when these myriads of mindless agents are combined in special ways, genuine intelligence emerges. So each of us is a combination of unthinking agents connected together and interacting with one another similar to the way our societies function.

Individually, Minsky's agents resemble computer programs; in concert, however, they could not be run on present-day computers. Conventional digital computers can only run a single program at any given instant; Minsky's societies would require the computer to deal with perhaps hundreds or thousands of cooperating and competing agent programs simultaneously. So Minsky points in two directions: toward a new theory of mind—that is, a new definition of humanness and how we function—and, at the same time, toward the design of a new generation of multiprocessing computers. Because the same concepts underlie both, the distinction between mind and machine becomes increasingly blurred. The two ultimately merge into one.

Psychologists and philosophers have been interested in our higher mental functions—memory, language and feeling—while biologists and physiologists have concentrated on our lower-order brain mechanisms—neurons, their connections, their chemistry. But until Minsky no one seemed to have any idea of how the lower brain mechanisms give rise to our higher mental states. His work stands squarely in this unknown territory.

Minsky assumes that minds are complicated machines and that intelligence arises from the confluence of simple, nonintelligent agents. His concerns are with what kinds of machines form our minds and how the agents interact. He seldom refers to computers or artificial intelligence, because present-day computers are inadequate to carry out his ideas. Similarly, he does not often refer to his agents as programs, since the multiprocessing or neural-net computers he has in mind will require quite different programs from those that run conventional digital computers; thus it is simplistic to call them programs. Nevertheless, with these reservations we will use computer and program terminology to describe Minsky's idea of the human mind.

Simple Things First

As we take a closer look at this new definition of mind, we need to start with simple things. Minsky concentrates on a few basic human activities that we all take for granted—one of which is a child playing with blocks. What Minsky discovers there he then extends into all areas of our mental geography, including language, learning and consciousness. And so this world of blocks can show us how the society of mind begins.

When a child plays with blocks, says Minsky, an agent called BUILDER is in control of the child's mind. BUILDER's concern is to make towers from blocks, but it needs help from many subordinate agents, like BEGIN, which chooses the place to start the tower; ADD, which puts a new block on the stack; and END, which decides when the tower is high enough. Each of these subagents needs help from additional subordinates; ADD, for example, calls on FIND, GET and PUT. Even lower-level agents find their tasks too complicated to deal with. GET has to call on GRASP and MOVE; PUT, on the same level as GET, likewise has to call on MOVE, as well as other such subagents as RELEASE. All these agents are linked together in a bureaucracy, at times organized into hierarchies and at times in heterarchies, as when a given agent must work for more than one supervisor. Already we see the influence of computers in the new theory of mind. If people familiar with computers were to stumble on this passage apart from its context, they would quickly conclude that they were reading about the construction of an industrial robot.

This simple presentation merely sketches all the complex interactions performed by various agents at different levels. A reader unfamiliar with the way computer programs interact might well ask how these agents know what to do when and with what. This is a valid concern not only for BUILDER but for the entire society of mind theory. Generally speaking, such detailed questions as to how information is passed back and forth between agents, or how they set each other in action, or even how they could be constructed have been answered. What we don't know yet is how these agents deal with each other—their social structure, in other words.

Minsky and his collaborator, Seymour Papert (a student of Piaget and the inventor of LOGO, the programming language used extensively in elementary classrooms), designed BUILDER during the late 1960s and early seventies at their artificial-intelligence laboratory at MIT. Their aim was to combine a mechanical hand, a television eye and a computer into a robot that could play with children's building blocks. It took years to develop MOVE, SEE, GRASP and the hundreds of other agents that go into BUILDER. They had to construct a mechanical hand equipped with sensors sensitive to both touch and pressure—sensors whose messages had to be interpreted by high-level computer programs. Their television eye likewise needed sophisticated programs to do what our brains do for us automatically: to discern the edges of the building blocks and to connect the lines and edges into three-dimensional representations. Additional programs had to be written that could use the fingers' sense of touch to verify what the eye had seen. Other programs computed the velocity and directional components of motion necessary to guide the hand accurately through space while, at the same time, the eye program checked to see if there was anything in the way. The highest-level programs enabled the robot to plan what to do. Others checked to see that what it planned actually occurred and corrected any mistakes. Minsky and his coworkers discovered that building with blocks, what every normal child does so effortlessly, almost thoughtlessly, requires thousands and thousands of little processes to anticipate, imagine, plan, predict and correct.

Workers in artificial intelligence have come to the inescapable conclusion that our common childhood problems are much more complicated than the sorts of problems adults consider hard—like puzzles, games or mathematics. We have the same sort of misconception when we rank low-skill jobs beneath those we think demand more intelligence and education. For example, let's compare the intelligence needed for a cashier to chat with us in the line, ring up our goods and pack our grocery bags with that needed for a scientist to write a research paper after having spent years plowing through volumes of math, physics and chemistry. If we had a trial of intelligence, cashier versus scientist, every single AI expert in the world would testify on behalf of the cashier. All the painful, conscious effort and seemingly complicated thinking we bring to the so-called hard problems is nothing compared to the incredibly intricate machinery necessary to accomplish ordinary common-sense things—most of which proceed flawlessly and beyond our consciousness or comprehension. Even if we argue that intelligence in such cases is merely a choice of wording, a matter of definition, AI researchers would adamantly disagree—and they have dealt with both types. Their opinion is born of hard experience.

As for us, how many sermons have we heard about the miracle of God's common grace and the wonders of his creation—the stars, the trees, the birds, the babies? We listen and forget. Even those of us who preach or teach are apt to admire an insight-filled treatise or the brilliant student rather than the lilies of the field or the janitor in the hall. Perhaps we suffer from a hazard of the trade, but even the most godless, arrogant AI researcher has a deep and conscious respect for God's not-so-ordinary creations. It does us no credit that we, who are to worship our Maker with all our mind and heart, should be so blind while others who do not have our perspective see more clearly.

But now that Minsky has introduced us to the complexities of the world of blocks and designed BUILDER, a concoction of programlike agents that acts in this world, it seems fitting to ask how could it really *know* how to build towers? And, if it does, exactly *where* would that knowing be located if none of the individual agents knows anything at all? In Minsky's thinking it's like asking, Where is the "run" in the runner? Each individual muscle "agent" dilates and contracts according to nerve impulses from a supervising command center. No muscle knows anything about running, and yet the total mechanism knows how to run—it depends on how we look at it. From the outside we would say that BUILDER is a composite agency that knows how to build towers, but if we look inside, we see a bunch of switches that turn individual agents off and on.

The Measure of Intelligence

Not all machines are created equal. Not all machines have the right stuff for intelligent behavior. Minsky and his colleagues would not claim that a car knows how to drive; it is not the right kind of machine. But if a car were equipped with a computer driver that could pilot itself through traffic and make decisions in accordance with its plans and goals, then we might have a different situation. It is not much different from our own brains driving us through all kinds of traffic, our minds millions of miles away and yet steering us safely toward our destination without our having one conscious thought about what we are doing.

We have what it takes for knowing, and so does BUILDER, at least in a primitive way. Taken by itself, BUILDER does not explain the state of mind of a child playing with blocks. We have to remember that it exists in a society of agents. In this society, BUILDER competes with WRECKER, each of which is controlled by PLAY-WITH-BLOCKS, which competes with PLAY-WITH-DOLLS and PLAY-WITH-ANIMALS, each of which is controlled by PLAY, which competes with EAT and SLEEP, and so forth.

The smallest agents in the society of mind do not exhibit what we would normally call mind, but they make up larger agencies inside our brains that do have the ability to deal with certain situations that we would regard as difficult, situations requiring mind or intelligence. Our systems of locomotion, vision and language are examples of agencies that have "mind." In turn, these larger agencies form a society of minds like the members of a family; each works with the others for the good of the whole, and yet each has its own mind and its own experiences that the others know nothing about. But is there a head of the family in this society of minds?

Not in the sense of a little person inside us who views and evaluates everything that we sense or do in the inner and outer worlds, answers Minsky. The idea of an inner, intelligent being doesn't help us understand anything; we would in turn need to explain how the mind of the inner person works. Minsky doesn't deny that all of us believe that we are singletons, but he does claim that this sense of oneness is an illusion, albeit a useful one. We have various models of ourselves, to be sure, but the "I" model does not control or direct our myriad mental agents. The "I" is a summary, a report, an abbreviated history of agents' activities past and present.

What about all those times when we decide to get a glass of water or raid the refrigerator? Doesn't the "I" do the deciding? Again, Minsky says no; there is no central self capable of making such diverse decisions. Our THIRST agent, in the water situation, has triggered its PLAN-TO-GET-NOURISHMENT subagent; our HUNGER agent, in the food situation, likewise calls on this same subagent, which in turn will call on the SEE, GRASP and PUT subagents to actually carry out the action. The point is that the THIRST agent sets in motion one decision, while a completely different agent that knows nothing at all of THIRST must set in motion the other. The "I," when it is conscious at all of a decision having been made, is a distilled summary of the diverse activities of thousands of different subagents that have done all the real work. As strange as it sounds, this is entirely consistent with readiness-potential experiments that show that we make decisions before we are aware that we are going to make them.

Our Sense of Self

All of which brings up the subject of consciousness, which is linked with our sense of self. Having argued that our awareness of being a single, unified self is a useful mental deception, Minsky asserts that consciousness is likewise not what it seems. We can see where this will lead. If there is no such thing as consciousness, in the sense of "I," then the argument that computers cannot explain the human mind or be humanlike because they are not conscious begins to fall apart. By Minsky's criteria, none of us is human in the traditional sense. This is certainly a major shift in how we view ourselves.

Consciousness, he says, is the name we usually give to certain processes that enable us to know what is happening inside our minds. But its reputation for self-awareness is not well deserved since it reveals little about what initiates our thoughts. Our conscious thoughts can merely signal us to steer the vast processes in our minds, much as we drive our cars without knowing or having to know anything about how the engine or the steering works. Minsky argues that consciousness is not concerned with the present but with the immediate past; it has to do with how we think about the records of our most recent thoughts. Thinking about thoughts is no different from thinking about external events. An agent can be wired to detect a brain-caused event just as easily as a world-caused event, since both are represented as signals in our brains anyway.

The roots of consciousness, says Minsky, lie with those agents that use and change our most recent memories. The little we know about how consciousness works stems from our limited capacity to record our recent thoughts. This is a necessary limitation; if we were to become more aware of what our brains were doing, there wouldn't be enough room left to do any further thinking. In addition, we would probably interfere with the proper running of our bodies. Who would really want to be conscious of the brain's work in keeping the heart pumping? Or, worse yet, be *responsible* for it? This explains why we become less conscious of some things as we become more conscious of others—our storage capacity is approaching its limit. Similarly, consciousness seems to flow in a stream; as we run out of space, our newer records displace the older ones, one after the other. This also explains why it is almost impossible to think about consciousness as we experience it. Each new thought displaces or changes our mental state. When we attempt self-inspection, we affect what we are inspecting.

Minsky's theory that consciousness is a succession of recent memory records passing through a machine of limited capacity may be a way of explaining how and why consciousness works, but it does not explain our sense of awareness, our experience of it. How could a machine ever be conscious in this way? Minsky's answer is simple. Since our brains are machines, we are asking if we ourselves could ever be conscious. The real question, then, is, What types of machines are capable of consciousness? and further, Can we build them? Minsky maintains that since we can provide machines with more and better records, brainlike machines are potentially capable of more actual consciousness than humans are. In other words, if consciousness is the key to humanness, computers may become more human than humans.

Some people have insisted that consciousness can only arise out of biological brains and that any attempt to create it in nonneural materials is doomed to failure. But imagine what would happen if each of our neurons were replaced with computer-type chips that would replicate the functions of each neuron in all respects. Since neurons are insentient and unconscious in themselves, consciousness must arise out of their organization and their social interactions; their *stuff* contributes nothing essential. Theoretically, it should be possible to build machines that have consciousness.

But even if consciousness for machines is not in the offing in the near future—or ever, for that matter—AI researchers question just how much consciousness has to do with intelligence. If being conscious is as shallow as they believe, all a computer needs to do is to emulate such functions as focusing or directing attention from one thing to the next or knowing when the unconscious systems can't handle a particular problem or situation. Then the grand project of creating intelligence will go on without mishap.

But what if an evolving system of programs, one that continuously grows in complexity, were suddenly to announce that it was fully conscious? Would we believe it? Since it would be so dissimilar to us, how would we judge its contention? We assume that other beings, whether people or higher animals, are conscious because they are biologically similar to us and because they certainly behave as if they were. Once again the Turing Test confronts us: we seem to be able to judge matters of intelligence or consciousness only on the basis of behavior or on what machines and people say about themselves.

Recall a student's comment about intelligent machines: "It's scary to think that we'll have to communicate with those things." It will not do to think that we have no worries about *conscious,* intelligent machines for some time; it may be more frightening to have to deal with intelligent, articulate machines that have no consciousness whatsoever—and yet are nevertheless considered human because the quibble over consciousness will have been neutralized by the new psychology.

There is nothing new, of course, about a thoroughgoing mechanistic view of the world. It's as ancient as philosophy and, in some instances, religion itself. But now we are confronted with it in a new way. We are not talking about an apple falling off a tree or the orderly procession of the celestial bodies; we're talking about our inner selves, our minds. We are confronted with an artifact that says, in effect, "What you see is you." Or so the computer mentality would have us believe.

But before we see where else the new view of humanity takes us and what we should make of it, we need to take a closer look at Minsky's theory.

The New Psychology

Gone are some of the older words of psychology, such as *generalizing, practicing, conditioning, memorizing* or *associating.* They are either too vague to be useful, or they are connected with theories that Minsky considers unsound. Because the revolution of computer science and artificial intelligence has given rise to new concepts of memory, learning and language, we need new words to reflect the changes, words such as *k-lines, level-bands, difference-engines, uniframing, transframing, recursion, predestined learning, recognizers, demons, suppressors* and *censors.*

Many people familiar with the older schools of psychology react to such a list with a mixture of horror and incredulity. Apart from a couple of words such as *suppressors* and *censors,* it would appear as if some mad scientist had started experimenting in the humanities building rather than in the lab. Thus many psychologists tend to dismiss the new enterprise out of hand or think that everything they have learned is destined to become hopelessly outdated. Such reactions are unwarranted, because no one knows if Minsky's particular terminology will survive. But one thing is certain: the *ideas* it embodies and reflects, taken from both neural physiology and computer science, will not only survive but will become standard fare in theories of the mind.

We must look closer at a few of these new words and ideas to get a sense of the new definition of humanity. First, *k-lines:* according to Minsky, whenever we solve a problem, have a good idea or have a memorable experience, we activate a k-line (short for "knowledge-line"), which is a wirelike structure that attaches itself to the mental agents that are active during or shortly after our experience of the event. Later, when we reactivate this k-line, we again arouse the agents attached to it, putting us in a mental state similar to the one we were in when we first created it. We can thus remember and apply what we've learned in one situation to another, similar one.

However, not all agents attach themselves to a k-line with the same strength. When we activate a k-line, certain weak agents are not stirred to the same degree as stronger agents. Let's look at kites, for example. Suppose that most of the kites we've seen before are red. When someone says the word kite, it activates our kite k-line. The weakly connected low-level RED agent leads us to assume that this kite is red. But if we're told that the kite is green, our RED agent is suppressed by our more strongly activated GREEN agent. Minsky calls these memory agents that can be temporarily suppressed by stronger agents "assumptions by default." Once a default assumption has been aroused, it stays active until there is a conflict, when it defers to a stronger agent, though always remaining at hand. Assumptions by default provide a business-as-usual background until a special event comes along; they give us some of our most common-sense knowledge and let us know what is usual, typical.

This brief introduction to k-lines and assumptions by default gives us a sense of how something equivalent to our mental states might be programmed on a computer. But what about goals or a sense of purpose? It seems altogether natural to ask how a mind machine, human or not, could have this sort of intentional mental state. Moreover, where do goals come from? We know that many of our earliest goals in life originate from our biology: get food, stay warm. Others come from our parents and various social institutions. We never do invent many new high-level goals, says Minsky. As we grow and become better able to control and predict our world, the subgoals we use in attaining our initial goals engage our attention, becoming independent and increasingly ambitious. Most of us are quite aware that much of the hustle and bustle of our lives amounts to "making a living" or "keeping up with the house"—not too far removed from "get food, stay warm." We also know that we don't live by bread alone; Christ's entry in our lives is one of those rare instances when we are challenged by totally new goals.

The Goals of a Machine

Are there processes inside a machine that could give the impression that it has a goal? Yes, Minsky claims. He calls such processes a *difference-engine*, though it has been known in the AI community since the 1950s by such names as "general problem solver" and "means-end analyzer." A difference-engine must have some sort of description of its goal. With a conventional digital computer this might be a string of 0s and 1s that represent some desired condition; in a neural-net computer or the human brain it might be a certain dynamic pattern of activated neural elements. Likewise, the difference-engine must have a representation of the actual situation—how things stand at present. The machine calculates the difference between the actual and desired situations and then activates certain subagents that try to reduce this difference. The difference-engine contains a subagent that makes it persist until the desired outcome is achieved, or until it is directed to do otherwise by higher-level agents or is thwarted by a competitor agent.

Do difference-engines have intentions? Do they really *want* things? Take a look at BUILDER, advises Minsky. If you remove its blocks, it reaches out and takes them back. If you knock its towers down, it builds them again. In a manner of speaking, BUILDER seems to want to build towers, but we really wouldn't mean the same thing as when we say a baby wants to build towers. But to Minsky this is a faulty assumption.

Perhaps BUILDER as an individual robot is not complicated enough to warrant our saying it "wants" or "intends." But if BUILDER were a minuscule part of a machine consisting of a dynamic society of thousands of layered and intertwined agents, including a language agency that could speak and create metaphors and other agents that could reason and learn from its mistakes, we would have far less hesitation in saying that this machine wants to build towers.

Keep in mind that according to the new psychology, no machine or person has a single, desiring, intending self. We are whatever agent has control at a particular moment. When a baby builds towers, its BUILDER has control, under the supervision of its PLAY-WITH-BLOCKS agent, which competes with the PLAY-WITH-DOLLS agent. Since there's not that much difference between a robot's BUILDER and a baby's, either may be said to want to build towers.

It seems that words have never been pushed to such extremities. But, says Minsky, we need not force ourselves to decide questions as to whether machines can have goals or not: "Words should be our servants, not our masters."[1] Indeed. If we don't like what words mean, he seems to be saying, change them or ignore them. Then, if we need not concern ourselves with such distinctions between people and machines, the computer mentality has realized its vision.

People learn, and learn to set goals, through rewards and punishments. Good grades reward hard work; a slapped hand punishes disobedience. Agents are likewise rewarded for successful behavior, but not in quite the same way that behaviorists envision. Minsky's notion of reward is similar to what a brain physiologist would call synaptic reinforcement. If a difference-engine has used agent A to arouse agent B to reach a goal, the effect of rewarding A will be to make it easier for A to stir up B in the future. But no simple system of rewards or punishments will result in significant learning. Once again, Minsky turns to the society metaphor, this time using a business situation. The following scenario describes the way rewards and punishment work in the society of mind; imagine the people in it to be like your mind's agents.

Alice owns a wholesale store. She tells Bill, her manager, to increase sales. Bill tells his salesman, Charles, to sell more radios, and Charles nets a whopping order. But the warehouse can't fill the order because radios are in short supply. Here we have a mix of success and failure, and the rewards and punishments are handed out in a fair-handed manner. Charles, the salesman, gets rewarded by Bill for doing a good job. Alice, who knows nothing about Charles's part in putting the firm in trouble, punishes Bill who should have checked the inventory. Presumably, if things had gone well, Alice might have distributed a bonus to everyone who had a part in increasing sales.

We might be able to teach a machine to learn something by distributing the rewards and punishments in such a manner. But how do we reward a machine? Human societies have developed different kinds of currency for rewarding actions—food, leisure or money. Similarly, societies of mental agents could use any substance of limited availability. For example, a society of neurons in the brain might be rewarded by a flow of chemical messengers that help develop the protein necessary to increase the strengths of various synaptic connections. Other societies in a computer or brain might use a currency that isn't electrochemical at all but a computed quantity, similar to money, that could, when accumulated in sufficient quantity, provide the machine with the wherewithal to expand its activities.

It is one thing to learn from success, but it may actually be more important to find out how a machine can learn from failure, as we do. Sometimes proven methods don't always work; the yeast fails and the bread doesn't rise, or the hollandaise curdles. We don't discard the proven just because it fails sporadically since that could result in general failure, rather than failure as an exception. It would be better to have certain agents on the lookout for exceptional circumstances—temperature too cool to activate the yeast, heat too high to mix the perfect hollandaise—than to change the whole method for each special case. Minsky calls these special agents *suppressors* and *censors*. A suppressor waits until we get an inappropriate idea and then prevents us from taking action on it, whereas a censor intercepts the states of mind that precede the thought. A suppressor says, "Don't put the bread in the oven at 2:00—it won't have risen." A censor says, "Don't even think about making hollandaise sauce on a day as hot as this."

The Universe of Demons

Suppressors and censors are a subspecies of a more general type of agent called a *demon*. A demon is constantly on the lookout for a particular circumstance, ready to intervene if it should occur. For example, suppose we give someone a gift. Usually people receive gifts gratefully. But a gift demon will be watching for evidence that the gift is being returned and then will look for signs that the recipient has rejected it.

This is similar to the way we have developed prohibitions and taboos in order to tell members of our community what not to do. We have censors, suppressors and demons permeating our society of mind that prevent us from not only repeating past mistakes but wasting time and effort. Minsky points out that though Sigmund Freud conceived of censors, writers seldom mention them in contemporary psychology; yet they play an important role in how we learn and how we think. It is interesting, however, that Minsky reaches his conclusions in a different manner from Freud. Along with his students and colleagues, Minsky found that they needed demons and censors to build machines that understand children's stories; demons help the reader understand how each phrase of a story leads to the next. Understanding itself is a huge accumulation of specialized skills and exceptions requiring a whole universe of demons. Minsky, in acknowledging that there are many difficult problems to be resolved in AI's demonology, wonders, "How much of the fascination in telling a story, or in listening to one, comes from the manipulations of our demons' expectations?"[2]

Freud believed that we form censors in our minds to serve as bar-
riers against forbidden thoughts, which explains one of the sources
of off-color humor. The effectiveness of a ribald joke comes from a
description that fits two situations or meanings simultaneously. Although the first meaning is obvious and innocent, the second is dis-
guised and forbidden. Our censors are too simple-minded to recognize the second, even though they are watchful and wary. Once the
first meaning has been firmly established, a sudden twist of a word
or phrase places the story in the context of the second, forbidden
meaning and our censors have been fooled. But never twice. The
deceived censor triggers an alarm, and we begin to laugh. Laughter,
says Minsky, is a mechanism that freezes our present state of mind
so that we retain in memory those records of events leading up to the
hoax. This gives us time either to strengthen an existing censor
against this state or to build a new one.

Although Freud was never satisfied that his theory explained why
we find innocuous nonsense jokes so funny and delightful, Minsky
thinks Freud was right all along. He merely failed to recognize that
ordinary thinking requires censors to suppress ineffectual and fruit-
less actions. Thus, we have logic and common-sense censors that find
inane thoughts as repugnant and forbidden—and as funny—as our
social censors find naughty ones.

People often say that the computer approach to mind can never
deal with humor. Yet Minsky argues that humor has a practical and
possibly essential role in how mind-machines learn. When we learn
things in a serious context, the connections between our ordinary
agents are changed; when we learn in a humorous context, the connections between our censors and suppressors are changed. Serious
situations involve positive learning while humorous ones involve negative learning. Both are important.

Can a computer have a sense of humor? A computer censor can
certainly be programmed to recognize when it has been fooled or
even when a censor of another machine has been fooled, providing
that the first machine had within itself a copy or model of the second
machine's censor. The whole business of humor could become quite
complicated, what with agents watching copies of other agents. In-

deed, when we start talking about copies of other machines or even copies of one's own agents within oneself, we begin to become involved with awareness and self-awareness. As we have seen, both humor and awareness are topics of current AI research, not only for the purpose of explaining the mind, but for the practical reason that computers will need to interact with people and learn from them, as well as from other computers. This means that computers will have to recognize and appreciate the way humans use humor. For example, one of the uses of laughter is to disrupt our own or another's train of thought; it focuses attention on our present state of mind—again so that censors may be strengthened or new ones created, according to Minsky. Laughter criticizes and corrects people's behavior without resorting to force or aggression. In short, laughter helps us learn.

Even with the current state of research, it is possible to create a program based on BUILDER that would laugh like a delighted young child at some of the mishaps in its world of blocks. In the not too distant future, something we say or do may set a whole network of computers around the world to laughing. It would be as embarrassing as being in a foreign culture when we uncomprehendingly make a blunder. "What did I say?" we wonder, our faces turning red. But certainly, we might argue, no machine could feel laughter the way we do—the way we double up, our sides aching, tears rolling down our faces.

In many ways this business of laughter summarizes the whole dilemma that computers present us. On the one hand, we have the feeling that no machine could reason, understand language, tell stories and have a sense of humor. On the other hand, either they can already do these things to a limited extent or, at the least, a plausible theory exists as to how they could do them. It's hard to argue that all of this is nothing but a shallow imitation of a human when a machine's sense of humor, for example, serves the practical purpose of helping it to learn and get along in the world—just as humor does for us. So how could we characterize a computer's sense of humor? Perhaps by saying "It's a bit weird—very intellectual, but without any mirth or feeling." Humor, which is both intellectual and emotional, seems to have lost the latter in machine psychology.

Emotions—Another Way of Thinking

We have followed Minsky from agents to censors to humor and, finally, to emotion. Any psychology worthy of the name must deal with
emotion. Not that Minsky tries to avoid the subject; on the contrary,
emotion plays a far more important role in the society of mind than
pure reason or logic. If we ask him, "How can a machine possibly
have emotions?" he will counter with something like, "Who's talking
about just machines? I'm talking about people, machines or anything
else that can be said to have sensibility." So let us see how emotions
fit into the society of mind.

Our culture teaches us that thought and feeling lie in two different
worlds. This is wrong, Minsky believes. They are worlds intertwined.
This seems like a startling pronouncement from a man who gives us
machines for minds. Yet emotions are not separate from thoughts but
are varieties or types of thoughts. We may think emotion is more
mysterious, more powerful and essentially different from thought, but
this is simply because we don't realize how complex and pervasive
ordinary thought truly is. When someone does something extraordi-
nary, we mistakenly credit the superficial emotional signs that accompany it, such as motivation, passion or inspiration. What should get
the credit, says Minsky, is the underlying, little-understood thought
process that did all the hard work.

Not that emotions aren't useful or real to the society of mind. In
infancy, the major agents of our minds are separate "proto-special-
ists," each concerned with a particular goal, need or instinct, such as
food, warmth, drink or defense. The demands of these proto-special-
ists make themselves readily known to our parents in the form of
emotional signals, the only way an infant can communicate its needs.
As we grow older, we develop administrative agencies that enable
these need machines to effectively exploit each other, as well as those
common sets of organs involved with touch, hearing, vision or various
body parts like arms and legs—all to find ways to get what they want
from the outer world. Our earliest emotions are genetically built-in
processes that control what goes on in our brains. But soon we learn
to overrule our single-minded need-goals with those that our parents,
teachers and friends provide us. By the time we are adults, all these

intermeshed systems have become too complicated to separate.

We may summarize it this way. Emotions perform various functions for us, and there are reasons why we have them. When we analyze their workings, we see that they are not that much different from thinking in their procedures, mechanisms and interactions. In fact, we have to deal with them functionally as a subspecies of thought programs. It is a common assumption in the AI community that when we come to understand what thought really is, we will also have understood emotions.

The question that Minsky poses is not whether machines can have emotions, but whether machines can be intelligent without them. He thinks that when we give machines the facility to alter their own abilities, we will have to give them something akin to emotions so that they can negotiate between the poles of dedication to a single goal on the one hand and a total lack of concern for anything at all on the other. Both extremes characterize what we mean by machinelike behavior. By using machine emotion to maneuver between them, Minsky intends his machines to be as *un*machinelike as possible.

Bear in mind that we are talking about a view of humanity, not whether machines can be made like humans—although it is sometimes difficult to discern whether the new psychology is talking about people or machines. This is part and parcel of what the computer mentality is all about.

We have taken a one-chapter tour through the society of mind, stopping at a few of the main attractions. But as in all such excursions we have missed much of what life is really like off the main route. However, our trip has provided us with a glimpse of a computer-age psychology and a look at what our children might be reading in their textbooks. Now that we have a basic understanding of the new view of humanity, we must begin to position ourselves in relation to it. The Christian view says that humans have a soul, and so we must confront and be confronted by the soulless information-processing view of humankind. First we must allow ourselves to be tested by it. In the testing, our own view might be informed and deepened.

7
REGAINING
OUR SOULS

The new computer psychology confronts us with questions we seldom ask. What is the self? What is the soul? Many might be surprised by the idea that we Christians don't think much about the self or the soul. Aren't we always concerned about that immortal part of our being? Certainly we believe in the soul. But the computer psychology asks us to consider our ideas in a way that hasn't happened since ancient times.

Despite our scientific and technological status in relation to those who lived millennia ago, we know little more than they. Most of what we know of the self and the soul we have appropriated from the past. We know that Christ arose from the dead, that he ascended into heaven, that he sits at the right hand of God and that we have the promise of life everlasting. This is the Good News that the ancients did not possess. But we know almost nothing about the soul itself—

search the Scriptures as we may. Is it the thinking part of ourselves? The conscious part? The core of ourselves in the present life that survives beyond death?

Thinkers from Plato to countless philosophers and theologians have been deeply concerned about the self and the soul. But do such arcane matters have a place in our scientific and technological age? Why should we be concerned with examining these matters any more closely than just to wonder about them from time to time? It would seem that talk of souls fits a different age—an age of togas, sandals and olive trees—or perhaps an age of cold stone cloisters and gargantuan theological tomes chained to wooden desks.

Yet, oddly enough, there is today more talk of self and soul than at any other time since the Middle Ages. Listen to what Minsky says about the soul after he has denied that a person's thought, will and decisions originate from a single center of control, the self:

> A common concept of the soul is that the essence of a self lies in some spark of invisible light, a thing that cowers out of body, out of mind, and out of sight. But what might such a symbol mean? It carries a sense of anti-self-respect: that there is no significance in anyone's accomplishments.
>
> People ask if machines can have souls. And I ask back whether souls can learn. It does not seem like a fair exchange—if souls can live for endless time and yet not use that time to learn—to trade all change for changelessness. And that's exactly what we get with inborn souls that cannot grow: a destiny the same as death, an ending in a permanence incapable of any change and, hence, devoid of intellect. . . . What are those old and fierce beliefs in spirits, souls, and essences? *They're all insinuations that we're helpless to improve ourselves.*[1]

Certainly Minsky has misconceptions about what most of us think of as our souls. But in a way Minsky has put his finger on something that is theologically sound. He claims that the idea of a soul conveys a sense that our accomplishments as individuals are not significant and that we are helpless to improve ourselves. Our accomplishments, apart from furthering the kingdom of God, do indeed amount to nothing. Furthermore, we cannot save or improve ourselves individually or corporately, no matter what our science and technology brings us in terms of lifestyle, health and longevity. But Minsky presents us with an attitude that all of us as Christians living in the computer age must now confront. There have always been scientists and philosophers who denied the soul, who claimed that there is nothing beyond the physical. Still, there has always been the mystery of self and mind that none of them could begin to explain. This mystery supported the notion of an immortal soul even apart from theological considerations. As long as there was mystery surrounding the self, our ideas of the soul could lurk about in the shadows, safe and unchallenged. Indeed, how many of our ideas concerning the soul come from "those old and fierce beliefs," as Minsky claims?

Back to Plato

One of the oldest sources of coherent thought about the soul is Plato. According to him, the human soul separates into a higher, rational part and a lower, irrational part. The rational part is primarily intellectual, but he seems to include such traits as gentleness, humility and reverence along with it—characteristics that we believe our philosophers and theologians should possess. The irrational part of the soul splits into something akin to what we would call will, along with certain emotional traits such as ambition, anger and righteous indignation, on the one hand. On the other hand are desires—for pleasure, wealth, food, sex and even for intellectual pleasures. Although all the faculties of the soul are separate, they exploit each other and cooperate to form a unified whole. Indeed, Plato in some sense anticipated Minsky's society-of-mind theory by likening the soul to the ideal city state. There are as many classes in society as there are functions of the soul. The philosophers correspond to the rational faculty of the soul and ought to be the rulers in any healthy state or soul; the warriors correspond to the spirit or will of the soul; the farmers, artisans and merchants represent the lower appetites.

But Minsky parts company with Plato in that Plato insisted that the soul is eternal, indestructible and indivisible. Minsky denies all of these. Moreover, Plato argued that since the world is basically rational, moral and just, there is a future life of rewards and punishments to rectify the imperfections of this life—a view acceptable to Christians throughout the Middle Ages and Renaissance. Since the material world and the body are transitory and have no absolute worth, the rational part of humanity, reason, is the immortal part of the soul; it seeks to escape from the prison of the body and contemplate the beautiful world of ideas, Plato's heaven. Here again we have a theme that Christian theologians were to appropriate for centuries. We will see in a later chapter that this same antisensual strain exists in the field of artificial intelligence.

There is a sense in which Plato's pure, disembodied ideas have been reincarnated today in the form of programs and abstract patterns of information—more real to the modern AI researcher than the crude materials through which they flow. There are differences, of course. Plato's pure ideas are immutable and exist apart from time and space, whereas the modern information theorist sees ultimate reality as process, as dynamic patterns of information unfolding in bursts of energy taking place in a matter of nanoseconds in a time, space and world beyond the reach of ordinary human experience.

The self and the soul are irrevocably intertwined in Western thought. When Minsky says there is no single, controlling self within us, we think that he has directly attacked the idea of a soul as well. He has challenged an idea that has its roots in the soil of our entire philosophical and theological tradition. But the matter goes deeper than this. Classicist and computer scientist J. David Bolter maintains that the Greek world view was superficial and complacent in comparison to Western European thought, formed as it has been by Christianity and its desire to get beneath the surface of reality. He writes:

In moral terms, it led to the Christian preoccupation with the human soul as something deep and mysterious beneath the façade of human behavior. In later, secular times, psychology took up where Christianity left off, exploring the depths of conscious and unconscious human experience.[2]

The computer mentality offers us a direct challenge. As long as we regard the self and the soul as more or less the same, the one a secular version of the other, we remain on safe ground. What we learned in psychology classes in college is essentially reconcilable with what we learned in church and Sunday school—psychological and theological language to a degree can be interchanged, as many Christian psychologists have shown. Let the mechanistic scientists say what they want about how our souls result from a bunch of chemical reactions; they still can't explain the self. And so we and the humanists close ranks and give each other mutual reassurances.

The Illusive Self

At this point the computer psychology presents Christians with its greatest challenge. It offers a metaphorical explanation of self and mind that it can potentially bring into reality on a machine. It forces us to draw the boundary between natural and supernatural, between body and soul. What if Minsky is right? What if our sense of a single, controlling, intelligent self is an illusion?

We daresay that almost every Christian will argue against this position, but not necessarily from an informed technical viewpoint and probably not even from purely theological considerations. What we may be defending is our humanistic sense of uniqueness. We should realize that an attack on the notion of the self and our inherited philosophical notions of the soul is not an attack on the gospel. What we in the twentieth century constantly sweep under the rug is the stark fact that Christ's advent and resurrection are scientifically unexplainable. We live in an age where mystery is to be exploited, dug out and converted into usable facts, information, goods and services. But there is no point to Christianity if it becomes a scientific or computational theory, at best a way of enabling us to add an ethical or human dimension to an increasingly impersonal society.

Computer psychology forces us to confront the situation without the benefits and reassurances of secular psychology. The human mind and the self have been among the few remaining strongholds in the ever-shrinking area of the unexplainable; we tend to equate the unexplainable with the supernatural and the sacred. For example, no one up to now has seriously challenged the idea that the mind or soul is the seat of reason. Many of us would agree with John Milton that reason, though it may err, is the essence of the soul. Take away the *uniqueness* of reason from the human being and you take away a good deal of the support for believing in the soul. A society of computer programs presents an explanation where mystery has previously prevailed. No longer is either the soul or the self necessary to account for our highest faculty.

Does it matter? We think it does. As Sherry Turkle's study points out, the computer raises these same questions in the minds of children. She maintains that children debate the metaphysical status of computers in a way that brings philosophy into everyday life. Since when have mothers, school teachers or even Sunday-school volunteers had to deal with such matters? But it goes along with what Bolter observes:

> Those of us who belong to the last generation of the Western European mentality, who still live by the rapidly fading ideals of the previous era, must reconcile ourselves to the fact that electronic man does not in all ways share our view of self and the world.[3]

Keeping the Message Alive

So how do we keep the Christian message alive for this generation and the next? We Christians have to allow for the unexplainable, no matter how reasonable we may try to be about our faith. Resurrection and salvation do not set easily with people brought up with cars, televisions, the good life, genetic engineering, space probes, heart transplants, nuclear bombs and intelligent machines. One can, of course, try to keep open the possibility of mind, spirit or soul by asserting that they exist in a separate world from the natural, scientifically explainable world. This is what the eminent brain researchers Wilder Penfield and Sir John Eccles have done; they are dualists in the grand old style.

Eccles, a Christian apologist and Nobel Prize winner, likes to have the connection between the two worlds right where he can see them. He points to an area in the top part of the brain and says, "Here is the place where the mental world meets the physical world, where the mental world sends information into the physical world." How reminiscent of the seventeenth-century dualist René Descartes when he pointed to the pineal gland of the brain as the place where the interaction of the soul and body occurs. But when you point to something as definite as that to explain the unexplainable you risk your credibility when someone at a later time shows experimentally that it just can't be.

The dualist view is an alternate position that people take in the age-old struggle to explain the mystery of the body and soul, the mind and the brain. But lest we think that such matters are entirely academic and that no one really cares, we should listen to Sherry Turkle's encounter with Frank, a computer-science major at MIT and a devout Roman Catholic.[4] Frank wants to become a researcher in artificial intelligence, and he worships Marvin Minsky as a hero. He thinks of the brain as a machine but also at the same time has a deep commitment to the idea of the soul. Frank conceives of the brain as a sensing machine capable of vision, hearing and tasting as well as being composed of various interacting computational agents that could potentially produce intelligence. But the thing about human mind-machines is that they are so complex that souls come to inhabit them. The agents of the mind are so delicately programmed that the brain becomes the "province of the soul." The soul can only interact through the hardware of the brain. "It twiddles a few bits here and there," says Frank. In this way the soul directs and controls our actions so that we are not just a collection of neurons in a meat machine.

Although Frank thinks of the brain as a computer and the soul as a sort of program, he doesn't see an absolute split between the soul and the brain. He imagines the relation of the two much as he thinks of himself at the console of a computer. He, the programmer, has a direct line to the complex internal processing, but there are times when he feels that he is "part of the machine," that he is both the programmer as well as part of the thing being programmed. He feels that he is building something that is also part of himself. In this way he is able to experience the relation of his soul to his brain-machine. He says:

It is like a programmer and a computer. There is a harmony. A fit. The soul is sometimes sitting there at the console, at least one part of it is, and part of it is in the machine. It is continuously aware of the state of the machine and can change any part of it at will at any time. So I like to see that as emerging, the soul is not just typing in, it's a spiritual thing which inhabits this computer.[5]

To a person unfamiliar with complex computer programs, this sounds like medieval mysticism, a kind of transcendental vision. But those of us who have worked with computers for hours and hours without a break have a pretty good idea of what he is talking about. We know how our minds become fused with the machine. Frank's analogy, intellectually peculiar as it may seem, carries a great deal of intuitive force.

But how does Frank reconcile his religious and computational views of soul and brain? If souls can only inhabit human computers, isn't the whole enterprise of artificial intelligence an impossibility? And why isn't AI a form of blasphemy in Frank's eyes?

Frank replies that souls have resided only in people because there hasn't been anything else up to now with the computational capacity fit for souls to inhabit. But if people can replicate their own computational capabilities in programs and machines "it may come to pass, if God allows it to happen, that after we connect together several trillion NAND gates or their equivalents, it may come to pass that some adventurous soul will decide to use that machine as its 'receptacle' in this universe."[6] And then, we wonder, will we need a new Incarnation? Or will these new souls be sinless?

How strange to hear Platonic and Neo-Platonic ideas from a student of high technology. We could easily imagine ourselves in the year A.D. 325 at the Council of Nicea or at the Council of Chalcedon in 451 hearing the debates of the church fathers concerning Christian theology and Hellenistic philosophy instead of students in the halls of MIT in the 1980s. How does it come about that a machine gives rise to theological controversy and something that so strongly suggests ancient heresy? We might tend to dismiss Frank's ideas as mere eccentricities, but this would show a lack of historical appreciation for the fact that they were among the most pressing issues engaging the minds of the foremost thinkers of Christendom six centuries ago. It also ignores the fact that these ideas are much on the minds of students today—students who will be tomorrow's intellectual leaders.

Stripping Away the Mystery

There is something else that makes Frank's ideas seem strange. What we are hearing is the idea of the soul stripped of its familiar psychological trappings. Why talk about a soul infusing the brain when we can think of it as something as nonmystical and safe as the conscious, reasoning, unified self? But we must remember that the new computer psychology has already dismissed our centuries-old notions of the soul and mind as illusions. Without these reassuring notions, supposedly settled once and for all long ago, we are taken to unfamiliar intellectual terrain. We believe that Frank's ideas, undoubtedly heretical and perhaps somewhat crude in that they are not tricked out in respectable philosophical jargon, will not appear as peculiar to succeeding generations as they do to ours.

Some things never change, and some problems never go away. The issues of self, mind, body and soul are still with us, though the computer has evoked them with an urgency that Freudian theory, for example, could not begin to approach. Turkle comments that it is widespread among the students at MIT and Harvard to think of their brains as machines and their minds as programs. But, someone might object, isn't this to be expected? These are secular schools; surely you won't find this kind of thing in Christian colleges.

Cheryl taught a course entitled "Christian Perspectives on Learning" at a Christian college with a strong philosophical tradition. The course was designed to acquaint Christian students with some of the values and ideological trends in contemporary society and to put them in the light of a biblical perspective. One of the readings was taken from Turkle's *The Second Self,* and Frank's ideas were part of it. For the most part, these students were freshmen and sophomore liberal-arts majors. To her surprise, Cheryl found that almost all of them thought of themselves in the same way that Turkle's students did. In fact, only one student—and he a computer-science major—argued against the view of mind as program. Most of the class sided with another computer-science major who argued with equal heat that the mind is nothing more than a complex computer system. Turkle wrote that she was surprised at what she found, and so are we. We have encountered what seems to be a kind of intellectual generation gap, and it cuts straight across both secular and Christian institutions. This gap makes itself known not just in how we do business or prepare for our careers.

It appears that those on one side of the gap look at themselves in a completely different way than those on the other side.

What the Soul Is Not

What do we make of this new theory of humanity? Where does it take us? There is nothing inherently wrong with the metaphor, that of regarding our brains as machines, no more so than regarding our arms and legs as systems of pulleys and levers. Indeed, the mind itself may be nothing more than what the brain does. Nor do we think that Christian doctrine is incompatible with the idea that a person's thought, will, decisions and actions originate from the activity of complex societies of agents and processes instead of a single, special part of ourselves called the self. But whatever the soul may be, it is not, as Minsky claims, a singularly frozen form that cowers out of body, out of mind and out of sight. Although many of the ideas and connotations we have of the disembodied soul are borrowed from Greek philosophy and mythos and are not explicitly derived from biblical revelation, we Christians believe in the resurrection of the body and life everlasting—which includes, in some sense, life everlasting for the soul. The unity of the body and spirit are central to both the Incarnation and the Resurrection. Christ's body is gone from the tomb, symbolic of the fact that we, like him, will take on new bodies.

Nevertheless, the computer metaphor of the mind is intriguing, and it will hold a great deal of power for Christians and non-Christians in the years to come. Unlike previous metaphors it can be tested on increasingly complicated machines; at some point it will be hard to determine whether we are talking about a metaphor or whether we have the beginnings of a crude model. The danger lies not in the theory itself, but in the motivation behind the theory. "The noblest activity," Frank says, "is to create vessels for the wandering souls. . . . You want to capture the essence of humanity. What I like about Minsky is that he seems to want to make a computer that a soul would want to live in."[7] Or as AI researcher Roger Schank puts it, "I have always wanted to make a mind. Create something like that. It is the most exciting thing you can do. The most important thing anyone could do."[8]

Creating a mindlike artifact is indeed exciting. Christians are entering the fields of artificial intelligence and cognitive science for that very reason. This in itself is not wrong. But there is a fine line between studying God's creation and wanting to become gods. Frank has stepped over the line, and so have others. How close to the line can one come without stepping over? Recall the words of Hamlet:

What a piece of work is a man! How noble in reason! How infinite in faculty! In form and moving how express and admirable! In action how like an angel! In apprehension how like a god! The beauty of the world! The paragon of animals![9]

A human being *is* a created piece of work, the most beautiful creature in God's world, the pinnacle of the chain of being, only slightly lower than the angels. But some of us are forgetting the first part—that we are *created* and by someone other than ourselves. The most important thing a person can do, indeed the sole reason for our existence, is to worship and glorify God; one short step beyond Shakespeare's description and we find ourselves creating idols after our own image. It is difficult for inquiring Christian students, especially in the sciences, to remember this in the excitement of discovery. Although AI researchers will not create a human mind, there is enough evidence to suggest that they will create an artifact which embodies a form of intelligence that may, in certain areas, exceed our own.

Our Place Is Lost

Intelligence is one of the reasons humanity has always been high on the chain of being, with God the Creator standing at the pinnacle. With intelligence embodied in a machine, the whole ordering system collapses and with it goes the centuries-old assumptions of the relation between people and God. It can be argued, of course, that the chain-of-being idea as an intellectual construct collapsed some time ago, but there is no denying that its intuitive and psychological forces are still very much with us.

We have lost a reassuring place in the order of things. As rational beings, we are no longer unique in the universe. This brings us face to face with the fact that we derive our specialness from God alone and not from any other source, which is hard for us to acknowledge without the belief in ourselves as uniquely rational. That we are made in the image of God has meant that we share intelligence with God, *the* distinguishing mark from all other creatures. Our rational faculty is about the only thing we can point to as evidence of God's image and how and why he has chosen to engage us. The only other explanation we can propound is that we have souls, but it is far easier to point to reason since we have little idea of what the soul is. Although the problems of reason and faith are nothing new, the real possibility of intelligent machines does put them in a different context.

This is the challenge for the thoughtful Christian—the new context. The older context for the study of our species was embedded in literature and the "soft sciences"; the new intellectual context lies in a technical, structured language of mathematical precision and logical process.

Professors in both Christian and secular colleges and universities are beginning to feel threatened by the arrival of a new breed of intellectuals who are acquainted and comfortable with computers, artificial intelligence and information processing. Some are adapting; that's why we see Christian college courses that deal with the computer revolution and AI. But many ignore the situation or try to explain it away with arguments that have decreasing validity and force for their computer-wise students. These professors feel as helpless and outdated as a blue-collar worker or a middle manager about to be replaced by a computer.

Yet contrary to some views, the older context still has relevancy in the computer age. We have seen how the computer brings up age-old theological problems and heresies. The role of Christian thinkers and apologists is to define and defend the Christian position to those within and without the community. We need theologians who will leave the dusty library stacks, put aside parochial squabbles and learn enough about the technology to come to grips with the issues. But they mustn't forget to place their volumes of Plato, Aristotle and the early churchmen on the table alongside their flickering terminals. There is a lot of theology going on in the halls of high technology.

As creatures, we are not unique by virtue of our intelligence alone, but the nature of our intelligence distinguishes us from both animals and machines. This leads us to the heart of the matter: the role of language in our understanding of humanity, computers and reality.

8
STANDING
BY WORDS

In the end, everything comes down to words. People finally reach the point where they exclaim, "Well, it all depends on how you define *intelligence* (or *mind*, or *body*, or *soul*, or whatever). We agree, and all along we have reiterated that what words mean, and the metaphors we use to explain ourselves to ourselves, is not mere linguistic hairsplitting. Wendell Berry, noted essayist, poet and critic, senses something else afoot as well, something beyond the quibbling over the meanings of individual words. He writes:

> My impression is that we have seen, for perhaps a hundred and fifty years, a gradual increase in language that is either meaningless or destructive of meaning. And I believe that this increasing unreliability of language parallels the increasing disintegration over the same period, of persons and communities.[1]

In other words, no longer can we count on all of us agreeing that *bread, stone* or *mind* mean certain things. Elsewhere Berry is more specific: "It may turn out that the most powerful destructive change of modern times has been a change in language: the rise of the image, or metaphor, of the machine."[2]

Berry is right. Metaphors matter. If a faulty metaphor informs our views, we will hold faulty notions. But it's more than that. We are not talking so much about the meanings of individual words, important as they are, but rather a wholesale shift in viewpoint concerning mind, meaning, understanding and reality—in short, the whole superstructure of language. This mechanization of language, and the concomitant reduction of mind to matter, has been going on for some time, but the computer and artificial intelligence are both the culmination and the starting point of a new enterprise. Berry sees this revolution as the very "uprooting of the human mind." As always, it takes a poet to capture a complex situation with a phrase or image that explains its truth and significance. Wade through all the technical and philosophical complexities surrounding computers and artificial intelligence; nothing conveys what is going on with more precision and poignancy than the uprooting of words, the tearing up, displacement and ultimate withering of the human mind. This chapter is our attempt to understand the computer mentality's part in this uprooting— the hows, wheres and whys of this enterprise

We begin with the computer mentality's view of reality and the role language plays in its construct. We will see how the computer mentality attempts to sever the connections between words and the objects to which they refer so that meaning has little to do with experience. After which we will see how the computer mentality deals with metaphors, so fundamental to our language, our psychology and our religious beliefs. Minsky, for one, is quite aware that he must deal with them if he hopes to explain the human being in terms of program. After accomplishing this much, the computer mentality feels that it is able to insist that feelings or emotions are close enough to thought and intelligence so that if we have enough understanding of the thinking process, it will not be difficult to give machines emotions— at which point the human-machine connection ceases to be metaphorical and the human mind has been uprooted.

At first glance the computer mentality's world view looks like ordinary reductionism—the attempt to explain everything and everybody in terms of chemical reactions or the interactions of subatomic particles. But the computer mentality is not really interested in these matters. What really concerns such people is the dynamic logic, the interactions of disembodied programs, those abstract structures that they believe underlie everything. Matter, machines, brains and whatnot are mere conveyances, the means by which ultimate reality is realized. The AI enterprise and its doppelgänger, the computer mentality, are more constructionist than reductionist. They want to *build* intelligence, language and mind from scratch, from thin air. Computers or brains are just the means by which they can experiment and develop what they consider to be those ultimate realities. Machines and people are different, to be sure, but only in incidental and unimportant ways; both are merely boxes that convey the real goods, the computer mentality's final reality: information processing.

When we hear "information," we usually think of solid facts; "information processing" suggests that someone or something is developing content, meaning and knowledge from the facts. But this is not what these words mean to information theorists or the computer mentality. To them, information processing is much simpler—and much deeper.

On the one hand, we have unconscious, unintelligent neurons. On the other, we have the conscious, intelligent mind, the outcome of the functioning of those billions of mindless entities. In between our neurophysiology and our thoughts, feelings and hopes, says the computer mentality, lies a hitherto unexplainable gap, the place where the mediations between the physical brain and the nonphysical thoughts of the mind occur. Those mediations can now be described as information processing, the manipulation of signals and symbols from one state to another in ever-increasing levels of complexity.

The mind-body problem is about to be solved, and its solution involves the structure and mechanisms of language, taking the "words" of language to refer to both signals and symbols. Nothing else is necessary. To the computer mentality, words in themselves have no *meaning;* they have only structure, as when they must hold certain positions in a sentence to ensure logical consistency. What the words mean in a sentence, what they say or what the speaker intends to say, is not actually relevant to information-processing theory. Not that words can't have meaning in the ordinary sense, but whether they do or don't is unimportant.

If information and knowledge have nothing to do with one another, if structure and meaning are torn asunder, it is a short leap to equating what the mind does with what a computer does. To the computer mentality there is no more of a mind-body problem with humans than there is with computers; the problem disappears in the gap between neurons and thoughts. Clear-thinking people will realize that the gap has been bridged by the mathematical structures of information processing, and only a few theologically befogged minds will be unable to make the leap.

Passing the Buck

There are many ways to look at language. What comes naturally to mind is the syntax-versus-semantics, or form-versus-content, view. Much of semantics and syntax involves buck-passing. But for computers, be they avant-garde multiprocessors or brainlike neural nets, the buck never *stops.* Information processing lies entirely within the buck-passing camp; human language can both pass and stop the buck.

A dictionary is a simple example of a buck-passer: the meaning of every word is shifted to other words. Buck-passing doesn't mean, however, that we are always chasing our tails. For example, the formal language of mathematics is a buck-passer par excellence. In mathematics we start with certain undefined terms, the empty "nouns" of the language, like point and line, and set up certain relationships between them, the "predicates," such as "contains." We combine the nouns and predicates to form the basic sentences called axioms, such as, "If p and q are points, then there is exactly one line that contains both p and q." These axioms constitute the starting point, the "givens." Now we can begin chasing our tails by creating new nouns, new predicates and deriving new sentences by applying the rules of logic to what has gone before—all of which must have their origins in those fundamental nouns, predicates and axioms.

The formal language of mathematics begins with things that have no immediate meaning in themselves. There is nothing in our experience we can point to and say "that is a point" or "that is a line." A point is not a round dot; it has no size or shape. Likewise, a line has no breadth and cannot be seen anywhere in nature. The only way we can talk about points and lines at all is to talk about how they relate to themselves, how they connect. Sentences in mathematics are not true in the ordinary sense of being able to verify them in the real world. They are true only in the sense that each sentence has been derived from other sentences according to certain rules. In mathematics, the buck never stops and pure mathematicians are proud of that fact. And they should be, considering how far buck-passing has taken them.

Computer programs, like mathematics, are buck-passers. But unlike mathematics, computers can be linked to the real world by sensors and are both active and reactive. But ultimately the machine, like the mathematician, transforms one meaningless string of symbols into another meaningless string by using certain precise rules. The following quote, from mathematician-philosopher Bertrand Russell, applies to computer programs and information processing as well as it does to mathematics: "Thus mathematics may be defined as the subject in which we never know what we are talking about, nor whether what we are saying is true."[3]

Since the computer mentality sees the whole world as a vast information-processing system, nothing can have any meaning by itself, but only in relation to other things. Listen to how Minsky passes the buck: "The secret of what anything means to us depends on how we've connected it to all the other things we know. That's why it's almost always wrong to seek the 'real meaning' of anything. A thing with just one meaning has scarcely any meaning at all."[4]

He explains that we cannot say anything about a single point—not because it is too complicated to explain, but because it is too simple; you have to have another point before there is anything to say at all. The same thing applies to our sensations. Touch your ear. What can you say? Not much, says Minsky. Now touch your ear twice in two different locations, and then touch your nose. Now we can say something meaningful. We can tell which sensations are most similar; we can talk about their relative positions or their intensities. Says Minsky:

> For just as there is nothing to say about a single point, there's nothing to be said about an isolated sensory signal. When our *Redness, Touch,* or *Toothache* agents send their signals to our brains, each by itself can only say, 'I'm here.' The rest of what such signals 'mean' to us depends on how they're linked to all our other agencies. . . . In other words, the 'qualities' of signals sent to brains depend only on relationships—the same as with the shapeless points of space.[5]

The Buck Stops Here

When Samuel Johnson wrote his dictionary, he talked about the difficulty of trying to explain words like *bright, sweet* and *bitter*—ideas or sensations for which there is only one word for one idea. Johnson was confronting the obstinate fact that language is not entirely relational; there are places where the buck does stop. Either you know what sweetness *is* or you don't. Sweetness, touch and redness are not like shapeless points in space. When we sink our teeth into a juicy piece of apple pie, we experience something more than our sweetness or toothache agents telling us, "We're here." Their qualities do depend on their relationships to all the other agencies of the brain, but they mean something more to us than we can say or explain. Because of this, they require unique words that cannot be explained in terms of any others. Yet Minsky claims, "Beyond the raw distinctiveness of every separate stimulus, all other aspects of its character or quality—be it of touch, taste, sound, or light—depend entirely on its relationships with the other agents of your mind."[6]

The buck slows down a bit with "raw distinctiveness" but then resumes its journey into "relationships." This is as close as the computer mentality will come to owning up to the sensual distinction between the taste of apple pie and a stab of pain. Herein lies another key to the whole issue of artificial intelligence and the computer mentality. Words are not the things they describe—but the computer mentality tries its best to make them so because its reality is all talk, all relationships, all buck-passing. So it must be if the computer mentality hopes to describe people in terms of information processing. But it also knows that it must deal with metaphor and its role in our understanding of reality.

Metaphors

One linguistic criticism of artificial intelligence is that it cannot deal with metaphors, that such refinements of language and meaning are completely beyond the scope of computers and programs. But Minsky believes that

> there isn't any boundary between metaphorical thought and ordinary thought. *No* two things or mental states ever are identical, so *every* psychological process must employ one means or another to induce the illusion of sameness. Every thought is to some degree a metaphor.[7]

It is difficult to take exception with such a reasonable and forthright acknowledgment of the extent and importance of metaphorical thinking—that is, until we realize that Minsky is using a degraded concept of metaphor. Or, more precisely, he is removing metaphor by saying that everything is metaphor, like saying that the color red exists because everything is red. Yet without something blue, how do we see red? Any true metaphor or any extended metaphor (parable) gets its charge, its ability to startle us into greater understanding, from a tension arising from an inherent contradiction: something is and is not something else—an uncomfortable position for the literal-minded computer.

But Minsky stresses the similarities, the *isness,* between what he calls a metaphor and that to which it is likened. There is an important reason why he must do so, apart from the computer's difficulty in handling concurrent isness and is-notness.

Metaphor is the language we use in talking about God, who is, to a degree, unknowable. This is why metaphor, true metaphor, the linking of the known to the unknown, is so important to us Christians. God is a king, judge, husband, shepherd, farmer, rock, shelter, brook. He is all of these . . . and he isn't.

Just so for parables, those stories, or extended metaphors, that explain an abstraction whose meaning, without retelling, would elude us. "The kingdom of God is like," says Jesus, the story of an importunate widow, a treasure in a field, a friend at midnight. And so we nod our heads and say, "Now it's becoming clearer." But not to Minsky, nor to the computer mentality, stuck as they are on isness and their abhorrence of the world of the spirit.

Even so, is it possible for computers to deal with metaphors? At present they cannot. But Minsky and his colleagues have a plausible outline for programming machines to recognize and make metaphors *as metaphors are understood by these people*—more literal than figurative.

Minsky himself acknowledges that his theories are not ready to be programmed and that the right kind of multiprocessing computers do not now exist. But he is working toward ways of organizing the programs of hypothetical multiprocessing computers so that he can cross-reference memory and knowledge structures between seemingly unrelated realms of thought and so produce metaphors. It is easy to see why he thinks that every thought is to some degree a metaphor. One gets the eerie premonition that someday in the not-too-distant future a whole school of literary critics will be comparing a rose and a beautiful woman in terms of how strongly their sweetness and delicacy agents have attached themselves to their respective k-lines.

As we mentioned, this in itself indicates a shift in how we view language and reality. What a metaphor means to us—holding in tension the literal and the figurative—is intimately connected to what reality means to us, as any biblical scholar or translator will insist. It is our key to understanding the Word of God and God himself.

Metaphor, information processing and programs all indicate that if we want to understand why humans are not mere information-processing systems, we cannot look to the complexities of computer technology only, but to language itself. Our words are the means by which we know and express our reality. But if our words are rendered meaningless by mechanization, as Berry suggests, it is but a short step to viewing ourselves as emotional machines.

At this point, it would seem as though we could dismiss the computer mentality's description of the human mind by simply saying, "Computers and programs can't feel or have emotions; so the human mind is not a collection of computer programs." But Minsky and company would rise up in arms. They maintain that feelings, sensations and emotions are as important to their theory of mind as any other—more so, in fact, than behaviorist theory, for example. Feeling is a type of thought involving relations and connections no different in any substantial way from rational types of thought. The problem is not that computers can't feel or have emotions, but that we don't really appreciate the complexity of thinking. Says Minsky:

It is a mistaken idea in our culture that feeling and emotion are deep, whereas intelligence, how we get ideas, how we think, is easy to understand. If you ask someone, "Why are you mad at your wife?" they might say, "Well, it's really because my boss was mean to me, and I can't get mad at him." It seems to me that people understand the dynamics of emotions quite well. But they have no idea at all to speak of about how thought works.

I think we'll be able to program emotions into a machine once we can do thoughts. We could make a something that just flew into a rage right now, but that would be a brainless rage. It wouldn't be very interesting. I'm sure that once we can get a certain amount of thought, and we've decided which emotions we want in a machine, that it won't be hard to do.[8]

Geoff Simons puts it this way:

We are learning to understand the character of emotion in traditional living systems. Emotion, like the purely cognitive processes (memory, learning, problem-solving, etc.), is an information-processing phenomenon. . . . Once this character of basic emotions circuits has been understood, it will be possible to structure emotion into artificial systems. Emotion will then evolve rapidly as one of the many useful survival strategies in computer organisms.[9]

If we try to point out to these people that feeling in a human being is different from the way they describe it in computers, they will answer, "In what way different?" They would argue that their information-processing model explains any apparent differences in terms of control, regulation, feedback, homeostasis, adaptation, survival and so forth—all mathematical, cybernetic, buck-passing notions. Although they use the same *words* we use to describe the human mind, those words are not rooted in the same soil; in fact, their words have no roots in human experience at all.

Standing by Words

There are places in language where the buck *does* stop—places that concern themselves with the interaction between a person's inner and outer worlds, of which touch, sweetness or pain are simple examples. The origins of these sensations might be described equally well by brain physiology or by agent-programs, but their meaning, as it occurs to our consciousnesses, does not come from building from simple things to more complicated "programs." These lower-level processes have no meaning for us in themselves. Meaning comes from the end result of all these interactions; at the same time it is the starting point of language, mind and reality. The simplest, most fundamental things for a human being do not begin at the bottom as they do for computers. The buck does not stop with neurons, transistors, nerve impulses or information processing. Rather, it stops much higher up, somewhere toward the middle of the complexity scale.

The quality of sweetness, for example, is a given for us; we not only know when something is sweet and when something else is sweeter, but we can distinguish it from bitter or salty things. It isn't merely a matter of distinguishing various tastes and their intensities; it is a matter of the pure and simple taste itself. Once we assign the word *sweetness* to our taste, we cannot translate it into any other word with the satisfaction that we have said what we meant to say. The buck has stopped.

The computer mentality cannot let this go unchallenged. It would argue that a computer's taste agents could analyze the ingredients of an apple pie and determine the sugar content. Its sweetness agent, just like our taste buds working with our brains, would announce, "This is sweet." Likewise, the computer would not be able to use any word except *sweet* to describe its finding. We scientifically minded people cannot give a scientific account for the difference between what sweetness means to a computer and what it means to humans. As soon as we try to explain the difference, we lose our way. We have passed the buck. We must face the fact that words like *sweetness*, where the buck should stop, have meaning for us unlike the meaningless points and lines of formal mathematics or information processing's strings of empty symbols. Language starts with the sensual quality of sweetness, not with any underlying activities of our sweetness agents or even our taste buds. And we can't prove this fact; we can only assent to it and assert it. We have to stand by our words. The workings of the human mind and natural language are in direct conflict not only with the design of computers and computer language but also with the three-century-old, bottom-up, scientific view of the way everything is supposed to work.

The inescapable conclusion is that people must take responsibility for their own experience and the use of their language, even as Adam did when he walked about the Garden of Eden naming the flora and fauna. Making the buck stop requires a moral act on the part of Adam's children to maintain fidelity to our language, ourselves and our community. We become fully human only when we stand by our words. The computer mentality, however, cannot or will not take that responsibility. Responsibility requires a moral act that even a sophisticated or brainlike computer program is entirely incapable of—because it is not made in the image of God.

When You Can't Stand by Words

Nothing would make us understand that we humans must stand by our words, and a computer cannot, than for us to become a computer—to put ourselves in its place, to imagine what its world must be. In his article "Minds, Brains, and Programs," this is exactly what philosopher John Searle does for us.[10] Few articles have caused more furor in the AI community in recent times. Searle quarrels with those who say that computer programs can understand human language or replicate human intelligence. Searle designed a thought experiment, subsequently dubbed the Chinese Room, that has become a classic statement of many of the main issues not only of contemporary AI but also of cognitive science, philosophy and theology. Here is the way to know what it's like to be a computer.

Suppose you don't understand how to read, write or speak Chinese. Further, imagine that you are locked in a room with several baskets of Chinese symbols along with a rule book in English for manipulating these symbols written by programmers who understand both English and Chinese. The rules tell you how to put symbols together in a formal fashion by the way they look. One rule might say, "Take a squiggle-squiggle sign out of basket number one and put it next to a squoggle-squoggle sign from basket number two." As you are sitting in the room, some other Chinese symbols are passed into the room, and you are given other rules for passing certain strings of symbols back to the outside. Although you have no idea what is going on, people on the outside are passing sensible questions into your room, and you are passing back sensible answers by using the instructions in your rule book.

After a while you become so adept at doing this, and the rules the programmers have given you are so good, no one can tell your answers from those of a native Chinese speaker. You have become a computer and, at the same time, have passed the Turing Test with flying colors. In order to make his point absolutely clear, Searle has some questions about your age and life history passed into your room—this time in English. You pass out your answers, also in English.

You have done such a remarkable job of passing the buck in Chinese that by all objective scientific criteria you understand Chinese as well as you do English. But from your subjective viewpoint inside the room, you don't understand a word of it. This would seem to show the difference between computer understanding and human understanding beyond a shadow of doubt. To the computer mentality it proves nothing at all.

What Does It Mean to Understand?

The computer mentality has many rebuttals for the Chinese Room argument. True, it says, you don't understand Chinese, but the *whole system* of characters, rules and you, combined, does. This argument seems blatantly absurd. A room with some baskets of symbols, a book full of rules and somebody to shuffle things around—this is understanding language? Yes, says the computer mentality. Computers and brains both work this way. Think of yourself as a neurotransmitter inside a brain instead of a person inside a room of baskets and rules. Your job is to tickle the dendrites so that they will cause the neurons to fire exactly in the same patterns as if the natural neurotransmitters were there. You will know what to do at exactly the right time and place, because the program, which has been converted into appropriate neurochemical configurations, will tell you. In both cases you are a facilitator of the flow of signals and symbols according to a set of rules. In both cases no one would expect you, a low-level functionary, to understand what is going on.

To argue that the Chinese Room does not understand Chinese is to argue that a native Chinese speaker does not understand Chinese—which is absurd, says the computer mentality. The reason for the seeming difference between the room and the brain is that we do not appreciate what goes into the rules for manipulating those symbols in the baskets. All understanding, including our awareness of ourselves and what we are doing, is contained therein, just as it is present in the circuitry of the brain.

This is only one of the arguments against the Chinese Room. Perhaps you are already formulating a counter-argument against it. Rest assured that the computer mentality will have a counter to your counter. Our position has been simply this: the buck stops with human understanding, even as it does with touch or sweetness. And we can't prove it. Language is not a neutral affair as is commonly held, nor is it shut up and closed off like mathematics. Our concern with language is not just a matter of defining individual words, because agreement can be reached and lines drawn. It involves the fundamental question of what we mean when we say "understanding words."

This is where the machine metaphor and information processing are uprooting the mind—if we permit it. If we allow language to become a buck-passing affair, we should not wonder that it degenerates into meaninglessness. If we do not exercise our moral prerogative of saying where the buck must stop, we should not be surprised at the disintegration of persons and communities. The computer mentality's version of understanding forces us to realize that there is no neutral, scientific view of language any more than there is of humankind itself.

One of Searle's most able and distinguished critics, computer scientist and Pulitzer Prize winner Douglas R. Hofstadter, is among the few people in information processing who realize this. In commenting on Searle's original Chinese Room article, he says:

> This religious diatribe against AI (the Chinese Room), masquerading as a serious scientific argument, is one of the wrongest, most infuriating articles I have ever read in my life. . . . I know that this journal is not the place for philosophical and religious commentary, yet it seems to me that what Searle and I have is, at the deepest level, a religious disagreement and I doubt that anything I say could ever change his mind.[11]

Hofstadter is exasperated because he cannot prove there is nothing more to understanding than buck-passing, any more than we can prove that the buck *must* stop. We maintain that language does not relate to our understanding in a computerlike fashion, but by the way we take active responsibility for our experience of the world, by the way we uphold our words—by our philosophical or religious stand.

9
PRESERVING
OUR
HUMANITY

There are many ways to show how our religious viewpoint determines how we use language, but recall what God says to Job: "Behold, the fear of the Lord, that is wisdom; and to depart from evil is understanding." We know that the computer mentality thinks any notion of God fictitious, but what about the other ideas—fear, wisdom and evil? Fear might translate into "caution," expressed as a set of numerical probabilities. Wisdom might become a flow of information through a series of decision points, accomplishing a predetermined goal. But what about evil?

No one would deny that emotion and reason are necessary ingredients of evil. As we have seen, the computer mentality claims both are simply matters of information processing. But how would the computer mentality explain downright viciousness or sadism? What can it say about evil of subtler origins—wartless and seductive visions of delight?

Any program or explanation of mind that supposedly understands language or human reality *must* know evil. But the computer mentality claims to know something by being able to program it—or at least explain it in information-processing concepts. So, how does one program a humanlike intelligence, one with will, desire and cleverness, without embedding in it the seed of evil?

The computer mentality's response is blunt: there is no evil. To say that evil exists is as wrongheaded as believing that the wind and stars are malevolent gods out to harm us. Anything we call evil, therefore, is an inconsistency in our basic assumptions, a slip in procedure, a bug in our program. Because we are information-processing systems, evil (or what people have called evil) is a malfunction that can be identified and fixed. All the harm recorded in history can be understood in terms of faulty technique. Theological notions are unnecessary, irrelevant clutter.

Evil Makes No Mistakes

We Christians believe that evil is beyond programming; it is a condition of being. Evil does what it does deliberately—with full knowledge of the consequences. It makes no mistakes, no glitches, no errors. It may behave rationally or irrationally, whichever serves its purposes.

The computer mentality, however, admits only to rules of behavior that read like this: if A, then do B and not C. To Christians, evil and sin are not reducible to cultural rules of behavior that people occasionally transgress. That is mere morality. No, we understand that humanity is evil and sinful by nature. We're up to our necks in it, one step away from asking the devil for a loan. Unless we accept this, we misunderstand the Incarnation. Christ did not come to help us fix our moral or ethical programs; he wasn't particularly interested in them. In fact, he chastised those who tried to keep their moral and religious programs operating in peak condition. To disregard evil, then, is to disregard what lies in the human mind and heart. We'll never find the fault in our programs that causes evil; evil is beyond rules and logic.

In a perverse way, this shows humanity's incredible complexity; a computer program, no matter how intelligent, is by comparison a thing of simplicity and naiveté. When people worry that computers will take over, that they will render us obsolete, they tacitly assent to the computer mentality's explanation of what it means to be human. We know we can't unplug the computer; its wiring will be intertwined in all aspects of human affairs—everything from science to business to government. But when we worry that superintelligent machines will control us, we underestimate ourselves. We can relax, confident that because we are unapproachably self-interested and sinful, we will always keep the upper hand.

The computer mentality will have to learn about evil and sin before it can hope to produce more than a makeshift counterfeit of the human mind. But this is the very thing it cannot do. Despite its claims, the computer mentality doesn't understand what *understanding* is all about.

If that is the case, what lies behind the computer mentality? What motivates it? Turkle maintains that the computer is a psychological machine, an evocative object, which is the reason for its strong appeal. In addition, as we have tried to show, the design of computers from simple on/off transistors up through ever-increasing levels of complexity to a facsimile of human language itself provides for some people an appealing model of the human mind. But there is a certain uncomputerlike streak lurking behind all of these thoughts.

From the Natural to the Artificial

To the computer mentality, the most important events in history are the creation of the universe (or its cyclic reappearance), the emergence of life and the advent of artificial intelligence. As a participant in the latter, it sees its ideas and work as cosmically significant. And though the computer mentality's new psychology may seem like old-fashioned scientism, one thing really is new: the way the computer mentality relates to nature.

Unlike previous claimants to godlike status, the computer mentality does not seek to fathom the secrets of nature; it doesn't seek to control or exploit it. Rather, it wants to escape from the natural into the world of the artificial, freeing itself of genetic constraints and becoming the creator and controlling force behind an empire of reason.

We are not saying that the computer mentality is purely intellectual, disdaining the senses; rather, biology and the body do not hold a high place in the scheme of things—they may even be hindrances. We have seen how the computer mentality strives to give life-status to computers and how it subsumes feelings and emotions under reason and thought. But where does this lead? No one puts it more clearly than Robert Jastrow, a theoretical physicist who joined NASA in its early years. Former chairman of the group of scientists who developed the first plans for the scientific exploration of the moon and the founder of the Goddard Institute for Space Studies, he is a thinker who demands our attention. Note the religious language in this passage describing his vision:

> The era of carbon-chemistry life is drawing to a close on the earth and a new era of silicon-based life—indestructible, immortal, infinitely expandable—is beginning. . . . The computer—a new form of life dedicated to pure thought—will be taken care of by its human partners, who will minister to man's social and economic needs. It will become his salvation in a world of crushing complexity.[1]

For Jastrow and others, *machina sapiens* will evolve far more quickly than has any other life form. Its evolution will be the result of an environment—provided by humans—that will directly change a computer's program. These changes will be passed on to the machine's immediate successors. At first the evolution of *machina sapiens* will proceed haltingly as AI researchers gradually learn about common sense and language. But there will come a point when a machine will take on an indisputable glimmer of life and genuine intelligence. When this happens, it will become extremely intelligent in a twinkling of an eye, and myriads of subspecies will proliferate by means of super-evolution. The brain could never keep up with the increased competition between humankind and machine. Jastrow's solution? If you can't beat them, join them.

Jastrow, however, does not mean a metaphorical union or a mere symbiotic relationship; nor does he mean that we necessarily have to fill our brains with biochips, those transistorlike devices made of organic material. He means for *us* to join *them*—that scientists will some-day know enough to make this union a literal one:

> When the brain sciences reach this point, a bold scientist will be able to tap the contents of his mind and transfer them into the metallic lattices of a computer. Because mind is the essence of being, it can be said that this scientist has entered the computer, and that he now dwells in it. . . . At last the human brain, en-sconced in a computer, has been liberated from the weakness of the mortal flesh.[2]

(Note again the religious language and the machine-and-man parody of the "vine and branches" metaphor in John 15—we in him, he in us.)

Such a life form could live forever, housed in indestructible silicon and metal, free from the inevitable life-and-death cycle of a biological organism. A thousand years will be as a day to brains living in com-puter bodies. Jastrow believes that other forms of life in the universe have already passed through the phase we are now entering—long ago having unlocked the secrets of the brain and taken the fateful (fatal?) step of joining a machine: "In countless solar systems science has created a race of immortals, and the exodus has begun."[3]

Heady stuff, isn't it? Once again, we must remember that whether all this actually comes about is not of primary importance. What is important is the hope, the desire, the vision it expresses. Not all AI researchers would hold to all of Jastrow's views, and they certainly wouldn't endorse his theological language. Yet Jastrow's language is not all that inappropriate; the computer mentality does take a relig-ious position, and Jastrow's choice of words acknowledges this fact. Even so, it is a fact that most AI people would not admit.

A Closer Look at Those Religious Words

Having glimpsed the computer mentality's book of revelation, let's review some of the words it uses. The computer will *minister* to our human needs; it will be our *salvation; we will dwell* in it; we will be *liberated* from the weakness of mortal flesh; we will take on *immortality* in a chip; we will begin the most momentous *exodus* ever undertaken, led, as it were, by a machine Moses.

The words are familiar to all of us, yet taken in this context they seem obscene. Let's start putting things in perspective by turning once more to Walter Berry:

The Bible's aim, as I read it, is not the freeing of the spirit from the world. It is the handbook of their interaction. It says that they cannot be divided; that their mutuality, their unity, is inescapable; that they are not reconciled in division but in harmony. What else can be meant by the resurrection of the body?[4]

Berry's reflections show quite clearly that Jastrow's words have been uprooted from the very conditions that gave rise to them. Computers minister to our physical necessities, not to our spiritual needs; they will liberate us from the limitations of our flesh, not free our spirits; instead of reaching perfection in our resurrected bodies and becoming consummately human as God intended at the outset, we will become immortally inhuman. But the burden of the Bible, as Berry points out, is to remind, instruct and admonish us as to the reality of these mutual dependencies. The work of true intelligence, as exemplified and perfected in the mind of Christ, is to understand and restore harmonious interactions between them according to God's precepts.

The language of the Bible inherently contains these relationships. The relationship between God and us is seen as Father and children, Shepherd and sheep. Christ is the bridegroom or the vine; people should be brothers and sisters; farmers, trees, fruit, seeds and even the human body itself are all metaphors for the rich complexity of connections throughout God's creation. The language of the computer mentality works in direct opposition to our understanding of the connections between people, communities, nature and God. This danger is inherent in any technical, scientific language, confined as it is to its narrow speciality, but the computer mentality's language lays claim to all human discourse and all human reality.

What is the place of biblical language in a technological society? There is no doubt that the language of the Bible no longer captures the imagination. Is it merely that we no longer live in a predominately agricultural or pastoral society so that the message of the Bible is no longer heard? We think not. It isn't that biblical language has become old-fashioned or has fallen into disuse; rather the *connections* it represents, the realities to which it refers, have fallen into decline or disrepute. Contemporary society does not sustain the caring or nurturing relationships inherent in biblical figures of speech; instead, it is a message of self-centered success and temporary allegiances to people, family and workplace. The computer mentality, of course, has not been solely responsible for this state of affairs, but it provides the philosophical basis for separating language from experience, thereby cutting the already loose connections between nature, life and God. As Geoff Simons observes:

> In a philosophy where man himself is already viewed in mechanistic or materialistic terms it will be relatively easy to embrace the notion of machine life. In a doctrine that regards man as at least partly spiritual and possessed of eternal life there may be more reluctance to acknowledge the arrival of living machines. But it may be significant that the emergence of artificial life is happening in societies where traditional religious creeds are in decline. The burgeoning awareness that we are witnessing the emergence of a new family of living species must inevitably tend to strengthen the idea that supernatural components are redundant in any adequate definition of life.[5]

In a few strokes the computer mentality eliminates God from the picture of life.

There Are No People

Here we have encapsulated almost all the arguments of this book. The computer has fooled us; it has passed the Turing Test. Like a Chinese Room, it has processed information in a supposedly intelligent manner without the help of a human mind. We have no people standing behind the picture, or behind the words, to render fidelity or integrity to what is being represented. Understanding and appreciation of art or language are contained in the program. If we argue that it takes human intelligence to create such a program, we will have missed the point completely. The computer mentality's goal is to eliminate the human being so that the computer can take off on its own, released from the constraints of the flesh.

But we want and need to know that there is a human being behind the picture, behind the words. We need to know that art and words arise from the human condition common to both the artist and the viewer, the speaker and the listener. We eat, sleep, work, sweat, marry, have children and die. We want to know that the picture or story purporting to tell us about what this means has been created by someone who experiences the same things we do, even as God in Christ entered the condition of our lives. Otherwise, why should we look or listen?

By a similar token, what meaning would a computer-generated poem have for us? The computer mentality would argue that readers bring all the feeling and meaning to a poem anyway, that a poem means what it does because its syntax and diction stimulate certain responses within us. Once again the computer mentality seeks to disconnect us from each other by asserting that we are self-contained, self-referential systems. We did not accidentally use the word *obscene* in describing Jastrow's use of theological language. There is a sense in which computer-generated art and poetry is akin to pornography, one distinguishing feature of which is its reduction of people to objects. Pornography isolates sex from the totality of life. People disconnect their bodies from the wellspring of their beings—their hopes and joys, their childhoods, their families, their destinies. They become isolated, cut off from the context of humanity; they have conditioned their responses to be independent of the sources of their own personhood and that of others.

But computer-generated art, music, language and intelligence are not inherently wrong, so long as the connections between people, and between people and God, are faithfully upheld. This is what makes biblical language so relevant in our technological society. It speaks of care, nurture and responsibility—the antithesis of and antidote to the computer mentality's language of isolation, fragmentation and self-interest. The Chinese Room, Jastrow's vision of disembodied immortals roaming the universe or a computer painting are all metaphors for a world without people standing behind thoughts and deeds. They are also metaphors for a world without God standing behind creation.

Science writer David Ritchie simply states that the world doesn't need Jesus:

> What the world *really* needs is a better way of handling information, because information is all-powerful (a fact which the Bible, interestingly, acknowledges when it describes the Almighty God in terms of information units: "In the beginning was the Word, and the Word was with God, and the Word was God"). Without information, nothing can happen. But *with* the right information, virtually anything is possible. And by coming up with the proper information, one can turn want and war into peace and plenty. The question is, how and where to look for the information we so desperately need.[6]

Here is another statement of the computer mentality's religion. Our problems, it says, are merely external to ourselves and arise from a lack of information; our salvation hinges on our finding the *right* information. There is no evil needing redemption or evil that refuses it when offered. And here is the ultimate corruption: the Word—the Incarnation—has become Information.

This points to another difficulty that our technological age has with biblical language. For a lot of us the most interesting and pressing questions of life are how everything works and fits together. We want answers, solid information, not hints and maybes and wait-and-sees. If Jesus wanted the undivided attention and respect of the best minds, why wasn't the Sermon on the Mount a definitive lecture on brain mechanisms, consciousness, chemistry and physics?

But Jesus didn't offer us that kind of reality—not that he wasn't tempted. He rejected this approach along with Satan's other offers of world domination through feeding the masses, astonishing us by incredible feats or sheer military coercion. Instead he spoke to us in parables and paradoxes whose ultimate meaning can only be understood by the way he stood by his words—and died by them.

The Mind of Christ
Here is the heart of the problem—we are to live by the words of Christ that were the result of the mind of Christ, that mind which Paul commands us to have; yet Christ's world was so different from ours that it is difficult to imagine him sitting at a terminal or being con-

fronted in the temples of high technology by the computer mentality. And yet that is precisely what we must do. That is what having the mind of Christ looks like today. We must think and speak as he would, despite the differences in our worlds.

We can remember, too, that he did leave his example to follow. We know that he was born in a world of rules, procedures and religious algorithms—the world of the Law. We tend to think that his was a simple, nontechnical world. We forget about the large body of intricate knowledge developed over the centuries by astute technicians of the Scriptures. Although there was no computer mentality as such, Christ knew how to challenge a mechanical model of the spiritual life. Notice that he knew the complexities of the Law; he understood and could speak the jargon of the Pharisees. He responded to their attempts to trap him by entangling them in their own snares. He removed the argument from the narrow confines of premises, logic and conclusions and cast it in a broader context—from the letter of the Law to the kingdom of God. He did so through stories, stories that endure and are appreciated by believers and nonbelievers alike. In so doing he established the links between the known and the unknown, between everyday life and the reality lying behind it.

To follow Christ's example, we must first engage the computer mentality and learn its true language. Second, we must take responsibility for connecting the words of our faith to those things to which they refer. By doing this, we refute the information-processing view of language and reality. We assert that we are not locked in the Chinese Room, manipulating symbols that have no meaning beyond their self-contained logical connections. Third, understanding our world is closer to understanding a story than it is to processing information on a computer. There is a mystery here that we mustn't be ashamed to acknowledge: we are made in God's image. Christ does teach us how to live in our world, even as he did for those living in the past and for those who are to come.

But what does it look like, this living in the world? We always need examples, those people who live as Christ would. Several years ago, Michael Ramsey, then the archbishop of Canterbury, spoke at the University of Pennsylvania by invitation of the Philosophy Club. Many in the audience were graduate students and professors whose specialty was logical positivism, an analytic approach to mind and language very close in spirit to the computer mentality. We could almost see them licking their chops in anticipation of the canonical meal ahead. Ramsey, seemingly oblivious to this, delivered his address and then took a chair some fifteen feet behind the podium to await the questioning. Philosopher after philosopher, each using specialized language and quoting journal articles familiar only to a few specialists, sought to confuse and confound him. Yet he strode that fifteen feet each time, delivered his response in a ringing voice, then turned about and marched the fifteen feet back to his chair. Soon there were no more questions. The audience solidly applauded him and left in respectful silence.

Not many of us, perhaps, remember what he said, but some of us vividly remember how he said it. It was clear that he could speak their language, and it was also clear that he spoke another language, a language they understood even though they disagreed with it. Nobody proved anything in that confrontation, but it brought everyone to the place where each had to recognize that there comes a point, what we Christians would call an act of faith, where all of us must stand by our words.

The Problem of Mystery

And this leads to yet another aspect of biblical language that presents a problem for computer-age people, Christians included. There are places in the Bible that contain direct commands and clear-cut information, but an aura of mystery hovers everywhere, an all-pervasive and unmistakable sense that we are encountering the almighty God. And mystery is something that anyone living today has difficulty with; for the computer mentality, it is anathema. A mystery is not a problem to be solved, nor is it the same as the unknown; rather it has more to do with the *unknowable*—and this is hard to accept. We are down-to-earth people, suspicious of anything that smacks of mystery.

It is unusual for anyone living today not to share, at least in part, the general optimism that mystery will disappear, that we will eventually come to understand almost everything about the world. There is a sense in which Ritchie is right about information being behind everything—that it underlies all science, technology and economics. And though information may at times be meaningless, it is never mysterious. Yet Christ's resurrection, among other things, is a mystery; there is no way around it. No matter how much we would love an explanation, God isn't giving one. Our God is not the great clockmaker of the eighteenth century any more than he is the great programmer of today.

How can we deal with mystery? One way is to put science and religion into two separate, mutually exclusive domains—a polite arrangement that lets us go about our affairs without stepping on each other's toes. Or we might put mystery in a closet, feeling safe in bringing it out and dusting it off for Christmas and Easter. We are not comfortable with either of these expediencies, for things are not that black and white. There are always gray areas to contend with, as well as our nagging insistence that everyday life must somehow fit into the eternal scheme of things. We want mystery, and we don't. And so, what religion calls the unknowable, science calls the unknown. And life goes on.

We have argued that language stubbornly points to things beyond itself; it is not entirely self-referential. We maintain that any comprehensive explanation of mind and language cannot be neutral, that it must take a philosophical stand. Furthermore, the computer mentality's vision is more than a dispassionate philosophical position; it is, at bottom, religious, a worship of an all-embracing intelligence that has been uprooted from human experience, patterned after a machine and blown up into a disembodied idol that is neither human nor machine. It is a form of self-deification—a form of narcissism.

We must understand that when the computer mentality seeks to redefine humanity, it does so by turning ordinary language into technospeak, which not only introduces new words and ideas into common parlance but fuses a different meaning to those notions that shape our individual and corporate lives: life, understanding, intelligence, meaning, good and evil, and mystery. This reshaping of our language is taking place in our elementary schools, our colleges, our places of work and in our relationships. For Christians to stand idly by is to assent to the computer mentality's vision. It is also to avoid the mystery.

For what we Westerners have lost sight of, what we seem to have little appreciation for, is that mystery is like a larger version of a puzzle, the kind we are not supposed to solve but whose sole purpose is edification. The computer mentality's world consists of formulas for applying rules, for manipulating the right information. It is the world of the schoolroom, a place where only certain kinds of questions are asked and certain kinds of answers are expected—a place where unsolvable puzzles are out of place. To embrace mystery is to embrace ambiguity and paradox, a highly undesirable or even impossible condition in the computer mentality's reality. Yet, *all* of us are students of the computer age and graduates from a centuries-long, honorable, scientific tradition. As such, we are trained *not* to ask questions without answers or at least without the possibility of answers. And so we fail to see that mystery can move us to explore the context of our lives, to look into our souls, to seek those connections between us and God that we might otherwise overlook. Mystery stretches our understanding of life beyond the computer mentality's well-formulated, simplistic view; it forces us to embrace ever-larger wholes that eventually open into the incomprehensible majesty of God. Perhaps, then, the only proper response to mystery, as Christian novelist Madeleine L'Engle put it, is not answer, but awe.

APPENDIX
WHAT CAN WE DO?

A Guide for Parents,
Teachers, Professors,
Preachers and Students

How are parents, educators, students, researchers, theologians, pastors, counselors and writers to respond to the challenges of the computer mentality? How can we take a responsible stand in the information-processing age without being assimilated by it or scared away? Being alert to the issues is a big step in itself. Recognizing the differences and similarities between the brain and the computer, knowing how the computer affects people psychologically, understanding something about artificial intelligence—its definition of humankind and the fundamental role of language—all go a long way toward strong, passive resistance. What we can do to counteract the computer mentality, of course, depends on who we are and our particular circumstances. But we would like to suggest some more active steps.

For Parents

What we saw happening to our own children motivated this book, and so our suggestion comes from our own observation and experience: there is nothing, we think, that foils the computer mentality's agenda more effectively than reading—reading the Bible as well as works of good fiction. Parents should themselves read and see that their children read too. But, more important, we believe families should read aloud together, no matter what ages the children are or even if a family consists of one parent and one child.

Books and computers have a kind of magic; each has the power to draw us into interior worlds. But those worlds are quite different. Not that the inner world of the computer is bad in itself; indeed, it is an exciting and fascinating world, one of the great achievements of the human imagination. It is also a microworld—a place where time is measured in billionths of a second and space is malleable. Complete and closed-off, small enough to control yet big enough to surprise, this tiny world lies far beyond the limits of human perception, all the while offering an almost unlimited range of possibilities for action. Within this abstract landscape, the computer mentality plays God, seeing itself as the masterful hero in a cosmic morality play where good means making the microworld do its bidding—and bad means losing control. It is a world where there are no unpredictable people to contend with, a world far different from the world of literature— and reality. Instead of recognizing and respecting the limitations of the microworld, the computer mentality extrapolates it to the real world, where people become biological embodiments of information-processing systems, not that much different from computers. The computer mentality thus severs the connections between mind and brain, language and experience, thought and feeling.

The world of literature, on the other hand, constantly reminds us of these human connections, that people and life are not abstractions. Literature shows the protagonists in uncertain situations and explores how they resolve the conflicts. They risk, they win, they lose and— as all humans must—they die.

Some children will come to live in the computer's inner world to the extent that it becomes more real than ordinary life, while others will merely pass through it. None, however, will be unaffected. We are not recommending that parents keep their children from computers for fear they will lose their way. Neither are we saying that everyone who goes deeply into the computer world will develop a computer mentality. But the computer mentality's view of life quietly pervades our age. There is a fine line between regarding the computer as an extension of the mind and regarding the mind as an extension of the computer. And, as we have tried to point out, language forms the boundary between these views. Reading and literature are among the few things that have a power equal to or greater than that of computers to hold and shape the mind.

Everyone knows how important reading is for job success and getting along in the world, but reading is much more; it enters into a child's development, just as the computer does. It is our job as parents to prepare our children for life, to teach them responsibility, to tell the truth and to walk with God. To ignore the world of reading and literature is to relinquish one of our most important roles as parents— and we can't expect our children to get it all at school. Most teachers have to be concerned with functional literacy.

Yet, despite all we hear about how difficult computers are to learn, the world of reading and literature is often even less accessible. The written word must come to life in the mind of the reader; alone, the mind must create the action, events, people, thoughts and feelings. A reader cannot turn on a switch and begin to interact with a ready-made world; the world must be activated entirely by the contents of one's experience, by the links between words and what words refer to. Some children acquire this ability without effort; for others it is a struggle. It is up to us parents to make sure it happens.

There is something special, too, about spoken words. A storyteller talks directly to us, whether we're children or grown-ups. "Tell us about the time you caught the sixteen-inch trout." "Tell us about the time Grandma fell in the toilet." "Tell us about the time you got sent to the principal's office." Tell us a story, any story. Young children and teen-agers want stories. Oh, teen-agers may grumble when a parent tells what life was like thirty years ago—but they listen. Why else is Bill Cosby so successful? He's a storyteller, though he doesn't *tell* what it was like to be a kid; he *becomes* the kid in us. He is the story, our story. Isn't that part of the power that Jesus, the greatest of storytellers, has exerted on the minds of people through the centuries? The Word became flesh—the story walked among us.

If there is something special about reading aloud, something even more special happens when the family gathers round, which is the other part of our suggestion: read together as a family. Why does this work? Maybe everyone is on the same footing; instead of being children and parents, we are just people sharing the same experience. Or maybe it's similar to what Christ taught us when he said we must become like children to enter the kingdom. Whatever the reason, it connects the ideas and feelings of the characters to those of the family and from there to the larger family of humanity. So, get a book and read together. Although not all of us are born storytellers, we can become storytellers when we read a good book aloud.

This is all easy to say, not at all easy to do. Everything seems to conspire against it. Television, movies and computers are not the only culprits. There are the pressures of a two-career family, the time-consuming tasks of shuttling kids back and forth from babysitters, school activities, church functions, music lessons and dentists, all the while squeezing in the laundry and the shopping, and praying that the cars keep running—all this when both parents get home from exhausting, demanding jobs that drain both body and brain.

But reading, especially reading aloud as a family, is a miracle medicine: it cures a host of ills, not least of which is the disorder brought on by the computer mentality. How can we make it happen, given the harried and all-too-typical scene described above? We have found that it takes a firm belief in the notion that people have time to do what they think is important. For us, reading is important. We made a rule to read aloud each day for an hour or so—and we stick to it. It hasn't always been easy. Most of the time we read before bed, but we have read at lunch, after a movie matinee and on long trips. The number of days we have missed can be counted on our fingers. There have been times when none of us wanted to read, when the idea seemed absurd, when all we wanted to do was go to bed. Until the words began.

Another part of the rule is that we read a chapter of the Bible as well, usually last. Sometimes this arrangement jars the sensibilities. A section of the Passion after a Zane Grey shootout or a rollicking fishing tale by Patrick McManus seems more than a little incongruous. But this is no stranger than how the Bible fits in with life itself. If we wait for those solemn and reverential moments when it seems fitting to read the Bible, we would only read it in church. Sometimes we say something to tie things together, sometimes we simply let it be. The cumulative effect of reading the Bible day after day in all kinds of circumstances makes a strong statement: this is where we stand, and these are the words we live by no matter what the situation.

When parents hear about our rule, they wonder how we make it stick; they know what our schedules are like. We try to tell them what it has meant to us, how our teen-age sons couldn't wait to hear the next chapter of *Amy's Eyes*—supposedly a children's book—how they vied with each other to do the reading, how they planned for the next books to be read, how they protested when we offered to give up on Dickens because we had to stop and explain almost every other word. When we hear parents' reasons why reading together is an impossibility in their own families, we often wonder if the real problem is with the kids at all. It seems that one or both parents are unwilling to do it; a nice idea, they agree, but not all that important—though they never come out and say so. Sometimes it seems that they have lost contact not only with their children but with themselves. One thing seems clear: they have forgotten about instilling their values in their children or maintaining their connections with them and with humanity.

Elementary and Secondary School Teachers

Although the family is the most fertile place to nourish the roots of mind and heart with literature and the Bible, just outside the home lies the school, where children's minds and characters are also being shaped. Computers are everywhere in education—from computer games that purport to teach children the three R's to sophisticated applications in engineering, business, economics, communications, foreign languages, psychology, chemistry, biology, anthropology, history and the arts.

Out of the excitement and confusion that surround computers in education we can distinguish two things: the use of computers in learning and research, and the set of attitudes and beliefs that accompany it—the computer mentality being the most dominant. In a way this situation reflects the distinction of being in the world but not part of it. Being in the world of computers begins in primary and secondary schools. Educators must be aware of how computers affect children—their ideas of aliveness, their sense of competence and mastery, and their identities. Only perceptive and informed teachers can see the darker side of what the computer can do to a child. Teachers not only must be trained to use computers effectively in the educational process, they must also be informed that computers are not mere tools but psychological machines capable of shaping personality. Computers are not neutral; they shape and extend the imagination.

We don't advocate keeping children away from computers until they arrive at a less-impressionable age. For one thing, the computer mentality is no respecter of age. For another, we believe that computers can reveal an exciting mental landscape combining text, graphics, movement and sound. But we embrace computers in education with a condition: that children be led into the world of reading and literature as well, that this world should be as alive and real for children as the computer's world and, furthermore, that reading and literature must take priority.

Because children so often accept the world of computers more readily than the world of reading, teachers are greatly tempted to take the easy way out. Yet teachers must put books first. If the habit of reading is not established early, if the child's imagination does not come alive to literature by a certain age, these things may never happen. Coming alive to literature means much more than being able to read or comprehend facts or think analytically about printed material: it is an inner life. It fosters metaphorical thinking and teaches the delights of paradox—the very thinking computers cannot deal with, yet which is so prominent in Jesus' teachings and parables. So our recommendation to teachers is this: make sure that each child gets the opportunity to enter the world of literature, to roam about its landscape and feel at home.

Teachers of Higher Education

The use of computers in higher education for teaching and research is exciting and revolutionizing. Although this is not the place for a full examination of the possibilities, a few examples will indicate what is happening already. Computer-generated graphics, animated and in color, are used in art design; computers are involved in the rapidly expanding field of electronic music; in theater computers are used for set design, lighting and sound, as well as choreography. Programs simulate historical events—the computer recreates the background, the people and their attitudes, while the student takes an active part in decision-making roles. Similar programs exist for economic and business situations as well. But the issue is not how the computer can be used in education—no one denies the possibilities—but how it affects the educational process at various levels.

The most obvious level has to do with the value of resources. Those marvelous applications we mentioned above don't come about easily. It always takes more time, effort and money than anyone realizes to bring an application into being. And once in place, machine often takes over—its feats and programs becoming more important than the subject matter it is supposed to enliven. At a deeper level, there is the danger that what can't be computerized gets neglected. Not all topics in a subject lend themselves to computerization, and so students come to regard those as less important, with the result that the whole subject becomes distorted.

There is yet a deeper level, the level at which the computer mentality operates. Here the concept of information processing is carried beyond its legitimate confines, until there is no distinction between our creations and ourselves. Not only does the computer mentality say, "In the beginning was Information," it says that humanity is an information processor, a technology, a product whose parameters are completely determined by evolution, that master program driving all creation.

Our point is that the computer is not only a sophisticated mental tool, it is an environment. This environment is not inherently hostile; it can be nurturing—or it can be the opposite. And like the natural environment about us, the ground we walk on and the air we breathe, it goes unnoticed. So it falls on teachers of higher education to become conscious of the computer environment, to make certain its features don't go unheeded. But how? Here are a few suggestions.

One suggestion is that computer-science majors—indeed, all science majors who will find themselves using computers extensively—be required to take an upper-level course dealing with the broader issues that computers raise—questions concerning economics, ethics, philosophy and religion. It might be a seminar in which students research a topic and write a paper to present to the class for discussion and criticism. Guest speakers could be invited to lecture on specific issues. The class would encounter the computer mentality from many different aspects, and we predict that both teacher and students will be surprised to discover how pervasive and persuasive the computer mentality has become. Such a course is already a requirement in some Christian colleges—for example, Calvin College—but it takes dedication and perseverance on the part of the computer-science faculties to insist on the requirement. It's not easy to squeeze yet another course into the curriculum, even though it provides a natural way for students to integrate the liberal arts with their specialty. Moreover, computer-science majors often resist such a course. As one professor observed, it is a struggle to get them interested in anything other than programs and computers and, if there is to be any extra time, students prefer to fill it with yet another technical course that they think will make them more competitive in graduate school or on the job.

This problem is not unique to computer-science education, but it may be more difficult for computer-science majors to see the theological and philosophical implications of their discipline. Biology and life-science students, for example, are quite aware of the evolution controversy or the ethical and religious issues surrounding abortion. Physics students know their subject deals with the beginnings of the universe and its end, or that quantum theory shakes our ordinary notions of cause and effect as well as our assumptions about objectivity and reality. But computer science is seen as mere technology, philosophically and religiously neutral. Computers are regarded as tools, not as environments of the mind.

True, computer-science students are aware of certain ethical issues surrounding computers, such as invasion of privacy, stealing money from a financial network or computer viruses. And they know that computers displace people on the job or change the lines of authority in an office. Most of all they are quite aware that computers could accidentally trigger a nuclear war. Although they know that computers change our outer lives, they fail to recognize that computers change *people* and the way people think of themselves.

This ought to distress Christian teachers who train those who will carry us deeper into the information-processing age. Christianity is about people, their minds and souls—and, as we have tried to show, so is the computer mentality. It is imperative that those who are about to transform the way we do science and commerce must be more than technicians; they must be aware that in so doing they have as much, if not more, power to shape our inner lives than do artists, novelists, politicians and preachers. This is the new battlefield where the church will be contending with those ancient powers and principalities of which Paul speaks. Yet computer-science students seem the least likely people to carry on the fight, being more interested in what is wrong with a program than what is wrong with the world. But God has always chosen unlikely people for his work, and colleges must do their part in his work by assuring that their computer-science graduates understand the true nature of their calling.

But what of the general liberal-arts student? Fewer and fewer students perceive that the liberal arts have any value for them, measuring educational value by a starting salary. A course on the effects of technology in our lives, different from the one for computer-science majors but one in which computers would be a major component, offers a way for students to see that the humanities and social sciences are not only relevant to their specialties but to their lives as well. Such a course lends itself naturally to an interdisciplinary approach. An intelligent discussion of technology necessitates drawing on all fields, including history, sociology, psychology, economics, literature, the sciences and, of course, philosophy and theology. Such a course wouldn't get far before encountering the computer mentality.

Regular courses, as well, can expose the computer mentality. Literature professors are sometimes chided for seeing the cross in every story or poem. But perhaps all teachers ought to follow such an approach when it comes to the computer mentality. For example, a classicist and a historian might argue that computers have little to do with their fields. Yet J. David Bolter in *Turing's Man* draws parallels between Greek culture and the information-processing age, between Greek thought and the world view of the new Turing Man, a not-too-distant relative of the computer mentality. His analysis provides us with a different outlook on our own age, an age that seems to break with all that has gone before. Not only do his ideas provide a fresh perspective on the computer age, they also offer a novel way for us to appreciate and understand the past.

In psychology, theories of how our minds develop, how we learn and who we are, are more and more shaped by computer concepts and models, especially in the area of cognitive science. Although students may encounter this now only in introductory psychology textbooks, they will soon experience its effects everywhere. The information-processing approach has already provided useful insights and models for the area of learning disabilities and will be one of the most important thrusts in child psychology, educational psychology and developmental education. In the next few years researchers will gather more and more information on the effects of computers on elementary and secondary schoolchildren. This data will have to be analyzed and integrated into teacher-training programs. Psychology directly influences how we educate our children in the classroom and how we raise them at home. More and more the computer will become a factor, both as a theoretical model and as a practical tool, in making these connections. We should remember that Roger Schank, Seymour Papert and Marvin Minsky consider themselves to be psychologists more than AI researchers or computer specialists. We should remember too that they are also educators whose ideas are becoming more and more influential.

Likewise, it isn't difficult to see the computer as the focus of an introductory course in philosophy. If the brain is a kind of computer and the mind is a kind of program, aren't our actions as determined as a machine's? What is free will? Are we responsible for our actions? Is the interplay between computer and program an accurate description of the connection between body and mind? What of rationality and intuition, objectivity and subjectivity? How could a machine, either computer or brain, be capable of consciousness? Or look at the Pythagoreans, Plato's forms, Aristotle's causes, Leibnitz's dream of a universal logical calculus—almost everywhere we see the computer mentality. The computer raises all the central issues of metaphysics, epistemology and ethics. Again, think of Turkle's study. If a thing causes children to ask the questions that have challenged the most reflective minds throughout the ages, shouldn't Christian thinkers take a long, hard look at the thing?

Aside from dealing with the computer mentality in individual courses, colleges should promote conferences on computers and technology, using the computer mentality as a bridge for the humanities to cross over into unfamiliar territory. The topics could be quite broad. What do writers like C. S. Lewis and Charles Williams tell us about language and information processing? Are we trapped in a sort of Chinese Room when it comes to words and understanding? What role do technologies like writing and computers play in shaping our mental lives, our style of thinking or our awareness of ourselves? Or turn to education, or child-rearing, or the workplace. Such conferences would provide a lively forum not only for college students and teachers but for the larger community. Business people, teachers and homemakers want to make sense out of what is going on around them. They *are* aware that something is happening, but they can't put it into words. This is the challenge for Christian scholars.

Thus, Christians in higher education should seize the opportunity to put technology in the perspective of the humanities and biblical teaching, taking up the computer mentality's challenge. Should some scholars think they don't know enough, or feel intimidated by machines, remember that computers and the computer mentality are not about wires and circuitry but about ideas. Reading some recent books written for the educated public will supply all the background a person needs. Thinking with the computer and thinking with the computer mentality are not the same. Scholars in the humanities must help us discern the difference.

For Theologians and Preachers

Theologians and Christian apologists have written about science, of course, but the consensus seems to be that science is one subject and religion is another. This is too comfortable. We have seen that the computer mentality is not born of pure science; it is a philosophical, antireligious position that needs to be identified and challenged. Theologians ought not neglect an opportunity to make the church's presence felt in the modern world, as well as to minister to the spiritual needs of millions of Christians who encounter the computer mentality every day.

We're talking about people who never read religious books, let alone theology, yet bought Tracy Kidders's best-selling, prize-winning *Soul of the New Machine,* or who took their children to see the entire *Star Wars* epic. These people are more than idly curious; they want to know what God has to do with the world around them. They want to see the green pastures and the still waters in the shopping malls; they want to know they are more than superdroids. Writing theology is a difficult and painstaking task, but it must reach out and engage technology because there is more than machines and gadgets involved; there is commitment of mind and soul. Where these things lie, so ought the concern of theology lie.

And so, too, ought the sermons we hear. Who doesn't like a preacher to talk to us in language we understand, to name the things that bother us and to speak the words that bring the kingdom close? We are children of God, the sheep of his pasture, and the pastor is the keeper of his flocks. We gather together to repent and worship God; the preacher interprets Scripture, admonishes us to keep Christlike relations with our neighbor, passes the benediction and sends us on our way. We, though, are supposed to apply what we hear to what we encounter in our lives, minute by minute, hour by hour. One of the problems is recognizing what we're supposed to apply the Sunday sermon to. Some things are obvious—thievery, covetousness, adultery—the basic Old Testament ten. Other matters of the spirit are not so easy to discern, especially when it comes to computers and technology.

Pastors and preachers are inclined to leave computers and technology to the scientists, technicians and business people, not realizing that these instruments are matters of the spirit. To a degree, science is one thing and religion another, but computers—and what the computer mentality makes of them—link the two in a new way. The computer mentality has definite ideas about the mind and what it means to be human. Unlike traditional science, which works from the outside to the inside, this philosophy works from the inside out—which makes it a spiritual matter. As Jesus said, it is not what goes into a person that defiles, but what comes out.

A pastor may view the computer in the church office as a great way to ease the business of the congregation. That's not the way the computer mentality sees it. It looks behind and beyond the computer. It sees the computer, as well as the secretary sitting at the keyboard, as the outworking of an evolutionary code and looks ahead to the further emergence of mind and intelligence—when secretary and pastor are not all that relevant. Pastors can no longer rest with the notion that computers have nothing to do with people's souls or their relationships.

What we want from the pastor is perspective; we want to make sense of our world through biblical teaching. We want words of wisdom. A pastor must give people the sense that he or she is aware of the problems and has dealt with them. A pastor must speak biblical language and the language of technology—not jargon, mind you, but the real language of technology—the words, ideas and imagery that underlie the technospeak. We're not advocating a series of sermons on the computer mentality; nor are we suggesting that a pastor preach about it every week. But we do suggest taking every reasonable and fitting opportunity to reveal it through sermon illustrations taken from magazines, books, movies and TV advertisements. There is certainly no lack of material.

Unfortunately, not much has been written to guide pastors. One helpful book that has appeared, however, is Chris Wiltsher's *Everyday Science, Everyday God*.[1] Wiltsher, a British theologian concerned with training effective ministers in an age of technology, names some of the tensions that a world of computers creates for Christians—tensions that pastors must recognize and deal with if the church is to be a vital presence in the future. How, for example, do human frailties and weaknesses fit in a world of mechanical efficiency? Or love—so important to humans and their relation to God, but seemingly irrelevant to the modern agenda of efficiency and power? If intelligent machines are the next stage in the evolutionary process, what will happen to the biblical teaching that God has given us dominion over the earth? Are humans even the pinnacle of God's creation? How do we, as sinners, fit in a world where elaborate computer systems all about us never err, never forget our errors and are utterly incapable of forgiving us? In this kind of world there is no need for forgiveness nor anything capable of extending it.

Wiltsher is also concerned with the effect that machine images in everyday speech have on our notion of a personal God. The way we talk about God in "terms of majesty, omniscience, infallibility, instructions from on high" is not only limited or changed in the machine age, but isn't that much different from the way we talk about complex computer systems.[2] The fear of the computer may replace the fear of the Lord as the beginning of wisdom. Wiltsher suggests that pastors need to make a conscious effort to develop images and models drawn from the world of the machine and to extend them into the Christian life. They should take advantage of the contrasts to the Christian viewpoint that computer imagery affords. For example, people feel and love; computers don't.

When we use illustrations and imagery from the computer world, we must bear in mind that the fundamental issue between the computer mentality and the Christian view lies with the connections between language and reality. Only people are capable of making these connections by commitment, assent and intention. Only people are capable of standing behind their words. All human discourse is a moral act and not just a matter of information processing. We alone are creatures made by God in his image.

For Students and Researchers

Walking that fine line between being in the world while not being part of it is one of the most difficult tasks for the Christian. It is especially difficult for those Christian students and researchers in the fields of computer science, AI research and cognitive science who, by the very nature of their work, are most susceptible to the influences of a world shaped by the computer mentality. Every day they are tempted to admire and emulate people who have the computer mentality. Techno-centered people appear powerful, need-free, efficient and flexible; they are able to process large quantities of complex data and make intricate logical connections between them. They possess the qualities that business, science and academia value so highly and, in one way or another, compensate so handsomely. The intellectually curious student or researcher hears the ostensible message: understand the mind, extend its power and open up new domains of human endeavor.

Along with this intellectual mandate comes the inevitable commercial, the one we see on television and read in magazines: use the products of computer technology to get the job done better and faster or else lose your competitive edge. But the more insidious message is one of personal power, superiority, security, control of one's personal life and control over the lives of others.

We are not suggesting that Christians avoid logic or efficiency. Nor should Christian young people avoid the field of computers or AI research. Indeed, they must not. But they should recognize the computer mentality for what it is, understanding that it directly opposes the mind of Christ. So what do we see for students and researchers? We see, as with the archbishop of Canterbury, the image of the church, led by these students and researchers, striding forth to make its presence felt and its message heard in an intellectually hostile world.

Notes

Chapter 1

[1]"Toy Makers Dolly Up to High Tech," *Grand Rapids Press,* February 11, 1987.
[2]Sherry Turkle, *The Second Self: Computers and the Human Spirit* (New York: Simon and Schuster, 1984).
[3]Ibid., p. 156.

Chapter 2

[1]Alan Turing, "Computing Machinery and Intelligence," excerpted in Douglas R. Hofstadter and Daniel C. Dennett, *The Mind's I: Fantasies and Reflections on Self and Soul* (New York: Bantam, 1981), pp. 53-67.
[2]Ibid., p. 57

Chapter 3

[1]For further reading, see Eric Kandel, "Small Systems of Neurons," *Scientific American* 241, no. 3 (September 1979): 67. See also, Joseph Alper, "Our Dual Memory," *Science 86* 7, no. 6 (July/Aug 1986): 49.
[2]John Sinclair, "The Hardware of the Brain," *Psychology Today,* December 1983, p. 12.
[3]The following is adapted from William F. Allman, "Mindworks," *Science 86* (May 1986): 23-24; and Otis Port, "Computers That Come Awfully Close to Thinking," *Business Week,* June 2, 1986.
[4]Allman, "Mindworks," p. 24.
[5]A fuller discussion may be found in Yaser S. Abu-Mostafa and Demetri Psaltis, "Optical Neural Computers," *Scientific American* 256, no. 3 (March

1987): 88-95.
[6]Port, "Computers That Come Awfully Close to Thinking," p. 93.
[7]Hubert Dreyfus and Stuart Dreyfus, *Mind over Machine: The Power of Human Intuition and Expertise in the Era of the Computer* (New York: Free Press, 1986), p. 215.
[8]Hofstadter and Dennett, *The Mind's I*, p. 382.
[9]Ibid., p. 374.
[10]Adapted from John Hopfield, "Brain, Computer, and Memory," *Engineering & Science*, September 1982, p. 3.
[11]William Calvin, *The River That Flows Uphill: A Journey from the Big Bang to the Big Brain* (San Francisco: Sierra Club Books, 1986), p. 33.

Chapter 4
[1]If you would like to know how expert systems are being used in psychotherapy, you might like to read Christopher Joyce, "This Machine Wants to Help You," *Psychology Today*, February 1988, pp. 44-50.
[2]Edward A. Feigenbaum and Pamela McCorduck, *The Fifth Generation: Artificial Intelligence and Japan's Computer Challenge to the World* (Reading, Mass.: Addison-Wesley, 1983), p. 80.
[3]Ibid., p. 82.
[4]Dreyfus, *Mind Over Machine*, p. 35.
[5]Ibid., p. 91.
[6]See Otis Port with John W. Wilson, "They're Here: Computers That Think," *Business Week*, January 26, 1987.
[7]Roger C. Schank with Peter G. Childers, *The Cognitive Computer: On Language, Learning, and Artificial Intelligence* (Reading, Mass.: Addison-Wesley, 1984), p. 33.
[8]The following is adapted from Natalie Dehn and Roger Schank, "Artificial and Human Intelligence," *Handbook of Human Intelligence* (New York: Cambridge University Press, 1982), pp. 369-70.
[9]Schank with Childers, *Cognitive Computer*, pp. 84-85.
[10]Adapted from Hopfield, "Brain, Computer, and Memory," pp. 2-7.
[11]The following is adapted from James A. Anderson, "Cognitive and Psychological Computation with Neural Models," *IEEE Transactions on Systems, Man, and Cybernetics* 13, no. 5 (September/October 1983): 799-815.
[12]Quoted in Allman, "Mindworks," p. 27.

Chapter 5
[1]Adapted from Craig Brod, *Technostress: The Human Cost of the Computer Revolution* (Reading, Mass.: Addison-Wesley, 1984), pp. 101-20.
[2]Ibid., p. xiii.
[3]Ibid., p. 129.

[4] Turkle, *Second Self,* p. 323.
[5] Adapted from ibid., p. 45.
[6] Ibid., p. 331.
[7] Ibid., p. 54.
[8] Ibid., p. 63.
[9] Adapted from ibid., pp. 29-30.
[10] Ibid., p. 30.
[11] Adapted from ibid., pp. 122-26.
[12] Joseph Weizenbaum, *Computer Power and Human Reason: From Judgment to Calculation* (New York: W. H. Freeman, 1976), p. 116.
[13] Ibid., p. 115.
[14] Ibid., p. 144.
[15] Turkle, *The Second Self,* p. 156.
[16] Ibid., p. 211.
[17] Ibid., p. 218.
[18] Weizenbaum, *Computer Power and Human Reason,* pp. 209-10.
[19] David Ritchie, *The Binary Brain: Artificial Intelligence in the Age of Electronics* (Boston, Mass.: Little, Brown, 1984), pp.181-82.

Chapter 6
[1] Marvin Minsky, *The Society of Mind* (New York: Simon and Schuster, 1985), p. 79.
[2] Ibid., p. 274.

Chapter 7
[1] Minsky, *Society of Mind,* p. 41.
[2] J. David Bolter, *Turing's Man: Western Culture in the Computer Age* (Chapel Hill, N.C.: University of North Carolina Press, 1984), p. 217.
[3] Ibid., p. 218.
[4] Adapted from Turkle, *Second Self,* pp. 296-98.
[5] Ibid., p. 297.
[6] Ibid.
[7] Ibid., p. 298.
[8] Ibid., p. 260.
[9] Shakespeare *Hamlet* 2.2.

Chapter 8
[1] Wendell Berry, *Standing By Words* (Berkeley, Calif.: North Point Press, 1983), p. 24.
[2] Wendell Berry, *The Gift of Good Land* (Berkeley, Calif.: North Point Press, 1981), p. 113.
[3] James R. Newman, *The World of Mathematics,* vol. 3 (New York: Simon and

Schuster, 1956), p. 1577.
[4]Minsky, *Society of Mind*, p. 64.
[5]Ibid., p. 113.
[6]Ibid.
[7]Minsky, *Society of Mind*, p. 299.
[8]Quoted in Patrick Huyghe, "Of Two Minds," *Psychology Today*, December 1983, p. 34.
[9]Geoff Simons, *The Biology of Computer Life* (Boston: Birkhauser, 1985), p. 161.
[10]Originally published in *Behavioral and Brain Sciences*, vol. 3 (New York: Cambridge University Press, 1980), reprinted in Hofstadter and Dennett, *The Mind's I*, pp. 353-73. However, we are going to follow John Searle's account of his article in his book *Minds, Brains and Science* (Cambridge, Mass.: Harvard University Press, 1984), pp. 32-35.
[11]Quoted in Howard Gardner, *The Mind's New Science* (New York: Basic Books, 1985), p. 176.

Chapter 9

[1]Robert Jastrow, *The Enchanted Loom* (New York: Simon and Schuster, 1981), p. 162.
[2]Ibid., p. 166.
[3]Ibid., p. 167.
[4]Wendell Berry, *The Unsettling of America* (New York: Avon Books, 1978), p. 109.
[5]Geoff Simons, *Are Computers Alive?* (Boston: Birkhauser, 1983), p. 187.
[6]Ritchie, *Binary Brain*, p. 196.

Appendix

[1]Chris Wiltsher, *Everyday Science, Everyday God* (London: Epworth Press, 1986).
[2]Ibid., p. 53.

Suggestions for Further Reading

Abu-Mostafa, Yaser S., and Psaltis, Demetri. "Optical Neural Computers." *Scientific American* 256, no. 3 (March 1987): 88-95.

An excellent introduction not only to current research in optical neural computers and holograms, but also to the connections between memory, pattern recognition, random problems, the brain, neural networks and the conventional digital computer. This article points the way to the construction of the most brain-like computer we encountered in our reading.

Bolter, David J. *Turing's Man: Western Culture in the Computer Age.* Chapel Hill, N.C.: University of North Carolina Press, 1984.

A classics professor with an advanced degree in computer science puts the computer age in historical perspective in terms of our notions of time, space, language and memory. Although critical of how the computer may restrict our historical and intellectual vistas, he also contends that it offers a new paradigm for science, philosophy and art. Bolter's work is a compelling example of how the humanities can inform and correct the world view fostered by computer technology.

Brod, Craig. *Technostress: The Human Cost of the Computer Revolution.* Reading, Massachusetts: Addison-Wesley, 1984.

Brod, a psychotherapist, uses case studies from his own files to argue that the computer can limit our ability to cope with the complexities of human relationships. Computer-style thought and technical jargon diminish the richness and depth of our language, our ability to love, and hence our ability to become fully human.

Dreyfus, Hubert L., and Stuart E. *Mind over Machine: The Power of Human Expertise in the Era of the Computer.* New York: Free Press, 1986.

These long-time critics of AI identify five ascending stages of human skill acquisition from novice to expert; the digital computer, at best, falls somewhere between the first two stages. Although their critique of expert computer systems is devastating, they do suggest that neural computers may offer a way out of the impasse. Other problems, however, still remain.

Heppenheimer, T. A. "Nerves of Silicon." *Discover* 9, no. 2 (February 1988): 70-79.

A brief history of artificial intelligence researchers' attempts to duplicate the brain's pattern-recognizing ability on the computer, culminating with the development of neural networks. It presents a lively and readable account of how researchers are overcoming some of the limitations of conventional digital computers as well as older versions of neural computers. It includes a description of NETtalk, the neural machine that learns to read without being programmed.

Hofstadter, Douglas R. *Godel, Escher, Bach: An Eternal Golden Braid.* New York: Vintage Books, 1980.

The blurb on the cover of our copy aptly describes this massive, Pulitzer Prize-winning tome as: "A metaphorical fugue on minds and machines in the spirit of Lewis Carroll." Of particular interest is Hofstadter's idea of how consciousness and free will could arise in self-referential systems, human or computer, by means of strange loops or the entangling of hierarchies. Hofstadter says that he stands somewhere between the two extreme views that say mind is fundamentally unprogrammable as opposed to the contention that, with the right combination of programs, genuine intelligence can be created. He does not consider, however, neural computers in his work.

Hofstadter, Douglas R., and Dennett, Daniel C. *The Mind's I: Fantasies and Reflections on Self and Soul.* New York: Bantam Books, 1982.

A delightful and disturbing collection of whimsical stories and essays that use the computer metaphor and information-processing concepts to discuss the age-old questions: What is the mind? Who am I? What is the soul? How can mere matter think or feel?

Jastrow, Robert. *The Enchanted Loom: Mind in the Universe.* New York: Simon and Schuster, 1981.

A noted scientist's view of how intelligence evolved in brains and how computers are the next stage in its development. Intelligence is about to escape the confinements of biology and take on an indestructible, infinitely expandable form.

McCorduck, Pamela. *Machines Who Think: A Personal Inquiry into the History and Prospects of Artificial Intelligence.* San Francisco: Freeman, 1979.

McCorduck extols the vision and visionaries of AI, while regarding its critics, such as Weizenbaum and the Dreyfus brothers, as little more than incompetents. Although excessive at times, this book is provocative and gives a lively account of AI's history as well as an insider's view of its practitioners.

Minsky, Marvin. *The Society of Minds.* New York: Simon and Schuster, 1985, 1986.

This is must reading for anyone interested in the new metaphor of the mind as a dynamic society of programlike agents. Minsky's book is far-ranging and revolutionary, yet amazingly precise and detailed for such an undertaking. Many influential thinkers in both AI and psychology believe that Minsky has pointed the way to go in the study of mind for years to come.

Rose, Frank. *Into the Heart of the Mind: An American Quest for Artificial Intelligence.* New York: Harper and Row, 1984.

A lively and informative account of the day-to-day efforts of a graduate research team at Berkeley University to teach computers to deal with the complexities of the English language and to exhibit some ordinary common sense.

Schank, Roger C., with Childers, Peter G. *The Cognitive Computer: On Language, Learning and Artificial Intelligence.* Reading, Massachusetts: Addison Wesley, 1984.

An insider's perspective on how close computers have come in understanding natural language and being able to adapt to change or the unexpected. Schank candidly discusses many of the philosophical and linguistic problems that confront AI.

Simons, Geoff. *Are Computers Alive? Evolution and New Life Forms.* Boston: Birkhauser, 1983.

The chief editor of the National Computer Centre in Manchester, England, argues that we are witnessing the emergence of a new life form in the computer. He contends that the definitions of living systems are moving away from biological considerations toward information-processing interpretations and that machines are not only evolving limbs, senses and cognitive capacities, but the potential for autonomous action.

Turkle, Sherry. *The Second Self: Computers and the Human Spirit.* New York: Simon and Schuster.

After three years of field work involving thousands of hours of interviewing and observing 200 children and 200 adults, Turkle has produced a well-written, engaging study of how the computer culture is affecting our thinking about ourselves and of how we are beginning to regard the machine in psychological terms rather than computational ones. This book is about why this happens, how it happens, and what it means for all of us.

Weizenbaum, Joseph. *Computer Power and Human Reason: From Judgment to Calculation.* San Francisco: Freeman, 1976.

For years this book has offered some of the most influential and cogent criticism of the kind of instrumental reason that underlies computers and artificial intelligence. Weizenbaum examines what computers can do, what they cannot do, and what they should not be allowed to do. Although his evaluation of what computers cannot do is somewhat dated, especially with regard to the new neural computers, his analysis of how the rhetoric of the technological elite is corrupting our language, our thought and especially our judgment is invaluable.

Index